EXPLICIT INSTRUCTION

A FRAMEWORK FOR MEANINGFUL DIRECT TEACHING

Jennifer L. Goeke
Montclair State University

Merrill
Upper Saddle River, New Jersey
Columbus, Ohio

Library of Congress Cataloging in Publication Data

Goeke, Jennifer L.

  Explicit instruction: a framework for meaningful direct teaching/Jennifer L. Goeke.

    p. cm.

Includes bibliographical references and index.

ISBN 0-205-53328-0

1. Active learning. 2. Student-centered learning. 3. Teacher effectiveness. I. Title.

LB1027.3.G64 2009

370.15′23—dc22

                                                    2008033019

Executive Editor and Publisher: Virginia Lanigan
Editorial Assistant: Matthew Buchholz
Director of Marketing: Quinn Perkson
Marketing Manager: Krista Clark

This book was set in 10/12 Minion by GGS Book Services PMG. It was printed and bound by Bind-Rite, Robbinsville/Command Web. The cover was printed by Bind-Rite, Robbinsville/Command Web.

Pearson® is a registered trademark of Pearson plc
Merrill® is a registered trademark of Pearson Education, Inc.

Pearson Education Ltd.
Pearson Education Singapore Pte. Ltd.
Pearson Education Canada, Ltd.
Pearson Education—Japan

Pearson Education Australia Pty. Limited
Pearson Education North Asia Ltd.
Pearson Educación de Mexico, S.A. de C.V.
Pearson Education Malaysia Pte. Ltd.

Merrill
is an imprint of

www.pearsonhighered.com

10 9 8 7 6 5 4 3 2 1

ISBN 13: 978-0-205-53328-2
ISBN 10:   0-205-53328-0

For my mother, Linda Goeke, who was my first teacher.

CONTENTS

Preface   *xi*

Part 1   Getting Ready to Use Explicit Instruction   1

Chapter 1   What Is Explicit Instruction?   3
Direct Instruction (D.I.) Versus Direct Instruction (d.i.)   5
   D.I.   5
   d.i.   6
Explicit Instruction: A Meaningful Alternative   8
Plan of the Book   12
   Summary   *13*

Chapter 2   Who Needs Explicit Instruction?   15
Understanding Your Students   17
What Does This Student Need? The Role of Assessment
   in e.i.   19
Monitoring Student Progress   20
   Large-Scale Assessment   20
   Curriculum-Based Assessment   21
   Classroom Assessment   22
Assessment and e.i.: How Do They Fit Together?   22
Case Example: Julia   23
Planning for e.i.   25
   Writing Correctly Worded Learning Objectives   25
   Lesson Planning for e.i.   28
   Summary   *28*

Chapter 3   The Engaging Teacher: Dispelling the Boring
   Myth   29
Dispelling the Boring Myth   29
Teacher Presentation Variables   30
   Teacher Clarity   30
   Appropriate Rate of Presentation   32
   Teacher Enthusiasm   33
Case Example: Melinda   34
   Summary   *36*

Chapter 4   The Active Learner: Dispelling the Passive Myth   37

Dispelling the Passive Myth   38

What Is Active Engagement?   38

Student Engagement Variables   39

Active Participation   39

Procedural Prompts   42

Monitoring Student Understanding   43

Summary   46

Part 2   The Explicit Instruction Framework   47

Chapter 5   Preinstructional Set   49

What Is Preinstructional Set?   49

Gain Students' Attention   50

Inform Students of the Learning Objective   54

Use Informed Instruction   56

Summary   58   •   Review   58   •   Apply   59

Chapter 6   Preparing the Knowledge Base for Instruction   61

Activate Prior Knowledge   62

Review Previously Learned Skills   64

Preteach Key Vocabulary   66

Summary   67   •   Review   68   •   Apply   68

Chapter 7   Instruction   69

Cognitive Modeling   69

Guided and Independent Practice   73

Closure   76

Summary   78   •   Review   79   •   Apply   79

Part 3   Applications of Explicit Instruction   81

Chapter 8   Explicit Instruction in Literacy   83

The Importance of e.i. in Reading   83

e.i. and Phonemic Awareness   86

e.i. and Phonics   87

e.i. and Vocabulary   92

e.i. and Fluency   95

e.i. and Reading Comprehension   96

e.i. and Written Expression   98

e.i. and Handwriting   102

e.i. and Spelling   103

e.i. and Composition   104

Summary   105

Chapter 9   Explicit Instruction in the Content Areas   107

e.i. and Mathematics   107

e.i. in the Content Areas   112

e.i. and Study Skills   113

e.i. and Learning Strategies   115

Summary   116 • Conclusions   116

References   117

Appendix A Explicit Instruction Lesson Plan Format   125

Appendix B Weekly Block Plans for Explicit Instruction   127

Appendix C Explicit Instruction Checklist   129

Index   131

SPECIAL FEATURES

TABLES

TABLE 1.1 D.I. Versus d.i. 8

TABLE 1.2 Explicit Instruction (e.i.) as an Alternative 9

TABLE 1.3 What Is Explicit Instruction (e.i.)? 10

TABLE 1.4 What Is Explicit in Explicit Instruction (e.i.)? 11

TABLE 2.1 Matching Assessment to Basic Skills in Reading, Writing, and Math 16

TABLE 2.2 The Learning and Teaching Continuum 17

TABLE 2.3 Deriving Meaning from Assessment Data 21

TABLE 2.4 Distinguishing Between a Learning Objective and an Activity/Process 26

TABLE 2.5 Parts of a Correctly Worded Learning Objective 26

TABLE 2.6 Performance Terms 27

TABLE 4.1 Active Participation Strategies 41

TABLE 4.2 Procedural Prompt for Main Idea 43

TABLE 4.3 Student Answers and Corrective Feedback 45

TABLE 7.1 Examples of Guided Practice Activities 74

TABLE 7.2 Lesson Closure Summary Sheet 78

TABLE 8.1 Instructional Considerations for Phonemic Awareness 87

TABLE 8.2 e.i. in Phonemic Awareness 88

TABLE 8.3 Research-Based Conclusions About Phonics Instruction 91

TABLE 8.4 Sample Phonics Scope and Sequence 92

TABLE 8.5 Phonics Instructional Model 93

TABLE 8.6 The Four Types of Question–Answer Relationships 97

TABLE 8.7 Reading Comprehension Instructional Model 97

TABLE 8.8 Reading Strategies for Explicit Instruction 99

TABLE 8.9 Handwriting Skills and Strategies 103

TABLE 8.10 Self-Regulation and Self-Instructional Strategies for Writing 105

TABLE 9.1 Prompt Card for Addition of Decimals 109

FIGURES

FIGURE 1.1 The e.i. Framework 13

FIGURE 2.1 Julia's Reading Assessment Report 24

FIGURE 3.1 Interaction Frame: Teacher Presentation Variables 31

FIGURE 5.1 Gain Students' Attention 51

FIGURE 5.2 Inform Students of the Learning Objective 54

FIGURE 5.3 Use Informed Instruction 57

FIGURE 6.1 Activate Prior Knowledge 62

FIGURE 6.2 Review Previously Learned Skills 65

FIGURE 6.3 Preteach Key Vocabulary 66

FIGURE 7.1 Relinquishing Teacher Control During Instruction 69

FIGURE 7.2 Cognitive Modeling 70

FIGURE 7.3 Guided and Independent Practice 73

FIGURE 7.4 Closure 77

FIGURE 8.1 Suggested Language Arts Format (Based on the Four Blocks) 85

FIGURE 8.2 What Does e.i. Look Like in Practice? Phonics Lesson 94

FIGURE 8.3 What Does e.i. Look Like in Practice? Reading Comprehension Lesson 100

FIGURE 9.1 What Does e.i. Look Like in Practice? Secondary Algebra Lesson 110

PREFACE

Robert was a student in my first second-grade class. His mother brought him to meet me one day as I was excitedly preparing my new classroom. She sheepishly introduced him: "This is Robert. He can't read." I assured Robert's mother that my approach to teaching would get Robert reading. He probably lacked confidence and needed a caring teacher who could change his attitude toward reading. I was trained by some of the most prominent people in the field of literacy, so I was more than prepared to deal with Robert's difficulties. In my class, reading would be fun.

As the year progressed, Robert's attitude toward reading did not change. In fact, it got worse. It got so bad by the spring of that year that Robert went from an introverted, sullen boy to a full-fledged behavior problem. One day, after I had repeatedly asked him to take out a book and begin reading, he took off his shoes, tied them together, and threw them at me, yelling, "I can't read!" It literally took Robert to hit me over the head with his shoes for me to realize that he did not need me to change his attitude or boost his confidence; he needed me to teach him *how to read*. I am embarrassed, in retrospect, by my willful naïveté. I persisted in my belief that I was doing the best for my students long past the point when I should have realized that in neglecting their instructional needs, I was actually doing them harm. Robert would go to third grade having neither acquired nor mastered a single reading skill or strategy in my classroom. This was especially painful because I knew that the outlook for third grade—where the emphasis abruptly shifted from *learning to read* to *reading to learn*—was dismal for those who weren't competent readers. I felt that I had worked so hard. I had exhausted myself, staying in my classroom for hours after school devising creative learning activities and designing a rich literacy environment. I tirelessly performed everything that my teacher preparation had taught me was not only effective but also *right*, and yet I had failed—miserably.

My devastating experience with Robert (and several others like him) led me to a critical reconsideration of my approach to teaching. I discovered that my teacher education had developed only one extreme end of a full continuum of essential teaching skills and strategies. I knew how to create a warm, welcoming environment that offered many creative learning opportunities to students who already had the skills and motivation to engage in them. But I lacked any knowledge and skills to adequately—if not effectively—teach the students with learning disabilities included in my classroom, those like Robert who were not identified but who were at risk for reading failure, or those who simply needed much more structure and direction in order to learn well. How could I have completed an entire teacher education program and never learned how to actually stand up and deliver a *lesson*? During the next few years, I doggedly pursued every professional development avenue to remake myself into an expert—and truly inclusive—teacher. Along the way, I met many other teachers with similar experiences.

Now that I am a teacher educator—almost 15 years after my experience with Robert— my classes are still consistently full of teachers who are just like I was. They are hardworking, well-intentioned professionals who often feel like they are failing at their jobs. When I think of these teachers, I then think of the thousands of students sitting in their classrooms who find themselves in a similar situation: because of inclusion, they no longer fit neatly into the world of special education; general education either doesn't want them or can't figure out how to meet their needs.

The real world of schools has been growing increasingly diverse and inclusive since before I became a classroom teacher. Yet teachers continue to have two very distinct and conflicting views of each other. General educators are viewed as masters of the art of teaching, whereas special educators are masters of the science. General educators focus on big ideas like *caring, democratic, student-centered practice*, while special educators promote practices such as *differentiated instruction, universal design for learning,* and *functional behavioral assessment.* Big ideas can be seductive because they sound kinder, gentler, more child centered. As a young graduate student, I was swept up in them too. It is in contrast to these big ideas that explicit instruction "looks ugly" (Traub, 1999) to many teachers, scholars, and advocates. When some of my colleagues heard that I was writing a book about explicit instruction, they assumed by extension that I had abandoned my caring, democratic, student-centered values; nothing could be further from the truth.

I have, however, reconceptualized my idea of what it means to be a caring teacher.

For me, the overarching lesson of my experience as a teacher and as a teacher educator is that we cannot continue to conceptualize teaching as an enterprise devoted to the "normal" students in our classrooms and expect teachers to figure out how to tack on an accommodation for the exceptions. The question is not whether one kind of teaching is inherently better than another but rather how teaching practices can be combined to create the ultimate in caring classrooms: those in which all students experience warm, welcoming, enriching, and *effective* teaching. In addressing these concerns, it is essential to acknowledge that students with disabilities are not the only ones who will benefit from this type of teaching. Teachers who use explicit instruction say that students with and without disabilities learn to read (some more easily than others, of course). If more students learned to read early on in their school careers, fewer students would need special education and remedial services. The use of effective instructional techniques in the general education classroom might make special education placements for many students increasingly unnecessary. Intensive and sustained effort toward the acceptance and improvement of inclusive teaching is the path toward true social justice for all students. This book is my attempt to help teachers embrace explicit instruction as one part of the full continuum of teaching skills and strategies and, in doing so, to become more effective and inspiring than they ever thought they could be.

I wish to acknowledge the enormous debt I owe to those who contributed to the creation of this book: my graduate students in the special education programs at Montclair State University who consistently inspire me through their energy and dedication, including J. C. Simpson, Michelle Rivera, and Caralyn Canova, whose ideas, comments, and examples appear in this book; the brilliant and supportive comments of my cherished friend and writing partner, Kristen Ritchey, who actually thinks my obsession with explicit instruction is a good thing; and my husband, Jon Caspi, and my son Ezra, who just make me smile.

PART ONE

Getting Ready to Use Explicit Instruction

CHAPTER 1

What Is Explicit Instruction?

Over the past 25 years, competing educational philosophies and instructional models have often been described as "at war." The "reading wars" are a prominent example of how disagreements over different teaching approaches have characterized the instructional landscape of schools. Teacher-directed instructional approaches have been the particular target of disdain among educators. Often, when working with a group of teachers or teacher education students, I will ask them to play a game of free association: "When I say the words *explicit instruction*, what words come immediately to mind?" Almost unanimously, they will say *boring, rote, mechanistic, robotic*—sometimes even *cruel* and *harmful*. I then ask them to examine the reasons why explicit instruction has garnered such a negative reputation, especially in light of the fact that it has been strongly supported by research in a variety of settings, for different types of learners. After all, many less well documented strategies have very positive reputations among educators.

Critical examination of this issue reveals that the misapplication and misunderstanding of the strategy rather than the strategy itself may have led to its demise among many educators. Problems result when any one teaching method is uniformly applied without regard for students' individual instructional needs. In the case of explicit instruction, classrooms are sharply criticized (and rightly so) in which students are passive learners, their voices rarely heard, in submission to large, uninterrupted swaths of teacher talk. Many new teachers, themselves victims of this type of indifferent instruction, enter the profession determined to do things differently. As a result, approaches to explicit instruction have been labeled "traditional"—what Rosenshine (1997) has called "politically and romantically incorrect."

As teacher-directed approaches fell out of favor among educators, more student-centered, constructivist methods gained popularity. According to these approaches, the teacher should not function as a disseminator of knowledge; rather, students must actively construct their own learning. The teacher serves as a facilitator or guide, arranging the environment in ways that maximize students' learning. A central tenet of constructivist approaches is the "minilesson." Teachers conduct brief periods of explanation in response to student questioning or "teachable moments." Labeling any direct teaching as "mini" might be interpreted as a response to the overwhelming amount of teacher talk that could be found in more traditional classrooms. It's as if educators wanted to say, "You can't accuse me of being one of those boring windbags! I don't spend much time directly teaching at *all*!"

The rise of constructivist methods meant that once again, many teachers (myself included) uniformly applied these approaches without regard to the consequences for some students. It takes a fairly bright, engaged student to think to ask the right question at precisely the right moment. What about those students who are so lost that they don't know what question to ask? "Mini" instruction may not be sufficient for them. In addition, teaching that happens only in response to teachable moments demands that teachers are prepared to provide any explanation in response to any question at any time. While many experienced teachers may feel comfortable and competent teaching "on the fly," less experienced teachers may need more careful planning in order to provide students with clear, accurate explanations. Although many teachers may feel more comfortable as a "guide" than as a "director," it is important to acknowledge that even in general education classrooms, many students actually *need* instruction that is explicit, directive, and intense, especially as they work to acquire basic skills and strategies. As Mrs. N, a fifth-grade resource teacher, wrote about her struggle to meet her students' needs,

> A great deal of content I must teach is based on the assumption that my students have certain skills, which they do not possess. When students are given strategies for accomplishing a task, they perform with greater success. One of the greatest issues of concern to me is that many of my colleagues do not want to spend time teaching something they feel students should have learned prior to entering their class. What difference does it make who teaches the student as long as the student is taught? If they do not learn skills and strategies they need, they cannot possibly move forward and access the content of any curriculum. Often my colleagues assume that a student can do the work, but chooses not to. This is difficult to assess. How do I know when a student is choosing not to work? If they are making that choice, why are they making it? Are they frustrated? I think most often the student is not taught strategies for how to react when they do not understand something. Also, they may not be taught how to generalize a strategy—that a strategy that was helpful in sixth grade may also be helpful in seventh.

Mrs. N's comments reflect a common tension between educators in inclusive settings. Mrs. N believes in the merits of providing explicit instruction across the curriculum—even to the extent of teaching her students affective strategies, such as how to express frustration appropriately. Others view themselves as grade-level or content-area specialists; bringing students "up to speed" is outside their realm of responsibility or expertise. Mrs. N's frustration highlights the need for inclusive educators to reconceptualize effective teaching across grade levels, content areas, and settings.

This book is called *Explicit Instruction* because it provides a contemporary middle ground for teachers who are wary of traditional direct instruction approaches but who acknowledge that many students—particularly in today's inclusive classrooms—need something *more*. The framework presented here is teacher led, but with a greater emphasis on the teacher–student transaction. In order to create a successful explicit instruction lesson, the teacher and students are joined in the instructional encounter; each has an important role to play in constructing learning. The purpose of this book is to challenge the view of explicit instruction as an outdated, mechanistic instructional strategy and to present it as timely, proven, and accessible. The explicit instruction framework is flexible and holds wide applicability for teachers across grade levels (elementary, middle, and secondary), settings (whole group, small group, general education, and special education), and content areas.

In this chapter, we examine the history and research behind teacher-directed instructional models. This historical perspective will provide the background and rationale for the explicit instruction framework. Contradictions of explicit instruction are discussed along with four assumptions that guided construction of the explicit instruction framework.

DIRECT INSTRUCTION (D.I.) VERSUS DIRECT INSTRUCTION (d.i.)

Teacher-directed instructional approaches have their roots in the behaviorist tradition of direct instruction. Direct instruction (D.I.), sometimes called expository, didactic, teacher-centered instruction or "active teaching," is a teacher-directed strategy in which the teacher transmits information directly to students. In a D.I. model, the teacher's role is to pass facts, skills, or strategies on to students in the most explicit way possible. This most often takes the form of a structured presentation that includes specific events of instruction, such as explanations, examples, and opportunities for practice and feedback. The D.I. format is a multifaceted presentation that requires verbal lecture and teacher–student interactions involving explanations, questions and answers, review and practice, and checking student understanding. The degree of student learning that occurs is directly related to the time a student is actively engaged in the learning process. Thus, efficient, effective use of instructional time and active student practice of content are key ingredients in D.I. strategies.

Two conceptions of D.I. are present in the literature. D.I. refers to a highly structured, ritualized, and scripted instructional model in the behaviorist learning tradition (Becker, Englemann, Carnine, & Rhine, 1981). The term "direct instruction" (d.i.) refers to the type of explicit, structured teaching outlined in the teacher-effectiveness literature (Rosenshine & Stevens, 1984). It is important to distinguish between these models of instruction since many scholars and practitioners have blurred the lines between them, and their differences have often become unclear. Research findings regarding these models cannot conveniently be taken together, as they espouse very different approaches to teaching.

D.I.

D.I. originated from two distinct lines of research. The first line of research focused on a set of models labeled *Direct Instruction*. D.I. models are based on the premise that through a teacher-directed instructional process, students can be trained to succeed. Behavioral theorists believe that it is not useful to speculate about internal cognitive processes since they cannot be directly observed or controlled. The curriculum and practice of D.I. are based on Skinner's (1968) operant conditioning theory, which stated that a behavior must be reinforced to bring about its regular occurrence. The "Direct Instructor," therefore, would conceive of teaching as a process of producing changes in students' observable behavior. These changes take the form of adding new responses to the student's educational repertoire.

Several key principles underlie D.I. approaches to teaching and learning. The central task of D.I. is to present students with the appropriate material on which to focus their attention and mental effort so that they will learn particular information, skills, and concepts. Skills and student performances of those skills are broken down into small units so that behavior and learning can be shaped incrementally. Initial teaching of any skill involves explicit, often scripted instruction on each step in the sequence. The teacher models behaviors before expecting students to perform them. The likelihood that students will generalize their learning to new situations is increased through engagement in practice consisting of real-life application and many examples from different contexts. Immediate feedback is provided on each step of a task. During demonstration and guided practice, the teacher provides redundant explanations, gives many examples, and provides sufficient instruction so that students can do the work with minimal difficulty. As student errors are minimized, the probability, frequency, and persistence of desired behavior are increased. A high frequency of student errors gives the teacher an indication that the presentation was inadequate and that reteaching is necessary.

The notion that a high percentage of correct, automatic responses plays a role in successful learning resulted from research by Samuels (1981) and others (Anderson, Evertson, & Brophy, 1979; Gersten, Carnine, & Williams, 1982; Good & Grouws, 1977). Teachers can minimize student errors by breaking instruction down into smaller steps and giving students instruction and practice to mastery on each step before proceeding. Students are provided with explicit demonstration of skills interspersed with checks of student understanding and teacher-monitored practice. In this way, the teacher can correct errors before they become part of the student's repertoire. A high frequency of correct responses is particularly important in the elementary grades. Research in D.I. indicates that the most effective teachers continue practice beyond the point where students are accurate, until overlearning has occurred (Engelmann & Carnine, 1982). When student responses are quick, accurate, and firm, the teacher moves on to a new question or topic, thereby maintaining the momentum of the lesson. Thus, D.I. constitutes a teacher-controlled method of instruction in which the learner is viewed as the recipient of information.

In addition to teacher presentation, D.I. is concerned with rigorous analysis of exactly how curricular materials are constructed. The key principle in the design of D.I. programs is that for student learning to occur, both materials and teacher presentation of those materials must be clear and unambiguous (Engelmann & Carnine, 1982). D.I. advocates argue that while commonly used teacher guides attempt to facilitate student interest and motivation, they fail to teach anything systematically. Different teachers will interpret directions such as "give an explanation" or "generate student definitions" in different ways. That is, how concepts and relationships will be taught is often left open to teacher preference or interpretation. Deviations in the way material is presented may result in confusion for low-performing students. According to D.I., instructional sequences must be detailed, precisely crafted, and implemented with fidelity in order to be effective.

D.I., then, is a teaching approach in which the level of teacher control is *high*. In fact, it has been criticized for being overly rigid and routinized and for ignoring individual differences among learners. For example, one of the most well known of the D.I. lesson formats is Reading Mastery (Distar Reading; Engelmann & Bruner, 1998). A highly ritualized, scripted, and phonics-based system of reading instruction, Reading Mastery calls for the use of tightly controlled vocabulary and complete mastery of each skill by each student in the group before proceeding to a new skill. Although many educators (especially those in general education) may feel uncomfortable with the level of teacher control imparted by strict D.I. programs, they have been shown to be effective for particular learners and contexts, including those with mild to moderate disabilities (e.g., Engelmann, 1980; Fabre, 1984; Gersten, 1985; Stebbins, St. Pierre, Proper, Anderson, & Cerva, 1977).

d.i.

A second line of research generated the term *direct instruction* (d.i.) to refer to the systematic, explicit teaching of skills and strategies. Many correlational studies found a relationship between student achievement and teachers' use of specific instructional strategies, such as teaching in small steps with student practice after each step, guiding students during initial practice, and ensuring that all students experienced a high level of successful practice (e.g., Gage & Needels, 1989; Good & Grouws, 1979; Weinert & Helmke, 1995). These techniques were intended to emphasize the teacher's role in maximizing the time that students are actively engaged in learning, thereby resulting in higher student achievement (Rosenshine & Stevens, 1984). This research was conducted primarily in basic reading and mathematics in the elementary grades.

Experimental studies also compared the achievement of students whose teachers were trained in d.i. strategies and students whose teachers were not. In other words, teachers were trained in the methods used by effective teachers, and their students' achievement was compared to that of students whose teachers did not receive such training (Slavin, 2000). These studies showed more mixed results. Some findings suggest that this is due to the fact that the recommendations from d.i. research make so much sense. That is, when studies have found no differences between teachers trained in d.i. models and other teachers, it may be because both groups of teachers already had many of the skills before the training took place.

Out of the teacher-effects research of the 1970s and 1980s, common teaching "functions" were abstracted that were associated with improved student learning. These were combined into a set of models labeled *direct instruction* (Rosenshine, 1995). These models developed as scholars examined the same research literature and generated similar but different models of d.i. (see, e.g., Gagne and Briggs, 1979; Good and Grouws, 1979; Hunter, 1982; Rosenshine, 1995). In general, all d.i. models share a common set of principles. These include teacher direction (rather than student self-direction or seat work); active presentation of information; clear organization of presentation, usually in the form of specific steps; step-by-step progression of instruction based on task analysis; use of examples, prompts, and demonstration; constant assessment of student understanding; effective use of time; and maintaining student attention. Guided practice, which follows the demonstration, allows the teacher to ask questions of students, check for understanding, and give feedback. Finally, students work on activities directly related to the new material during independent practice.

The general structure of a d.i. lesson takes on vastly different forms in different subject areas and at different grade levels. Teachers of older students may take several days to complete the steps of the process, ending with a formal test or evaluation. Teachers of younger students may go through the entire cycle in a class period, using informal assessments at the end. The sequence of a d.i. lesson flows along a logical path, from eliciting student attention and interest to presenting new information to allowing students to practice their new knowledge or skills to assessment (Slavin, 2000). This orderly progression is what characterizes d.i. at any grade level and in any subject, although the various components and how they are implemented will look different for different subjects and grades.

In comparison with D.I., d.i. is a generic teaching model rather than a scripted, fully elaborated program for teaching reading or mathematics. Unlike D.I., d.i. does not directly address issues of curriculum. Rather, d.i. is based on all available naturalistic research on classroom processes—research conducted primarily in general education classrooms, often with at-risk students. Low-performing students repeatedly show higher academic achievement when their teachers follow a consistent pattern of d.i. that includes demonstration, practice, and feedback (Tarver, 1992). The differences between D.I. and d.i. are summarized in Table 1.1.

Out of the history and background described previously, a set of contradictions emerged regarding d.i.:

1. Although many students across educational settings need some form of teacher-directed instruction, many teachers are reluctant to deliver it.

TABLE 1.1 D.I. Versus d.i.	
D.I.	**d.i.**
"Specific" teaching program	"Generic" teaching model
Based on operant conditioning theory. Teacher direction is very high	Based on research on classroom processes
Highly structured, scripted, and ritualized	Teacher direction is high
Targeted at adding new responses to the student's repertoire	Structured, explicit, clear, and controlled
Skills broken into small units	Emphasizes teacher's role in maximizing academic learning time
Behavior and learning are shaped gradually	Step-by-step presentation
High percentage of correct responses	Includes demonstration, practice, and corrective feedback
Skills are practiced to overlearning	Does not directly address issues of curriculum
Concerned with design of curricular materials	

2. Although d.i. has a strong research base, it is often degraded.
3. Contemporary views of learning hold that students must actively construct their own learning, yet many lack the prerequisite skills to do so.

These contradictions highlight the need for an alternative to traditional D.I. and d.i. models. In the current educational climate, instructional models are needed that are attentive to teachers' desires to actively engage students in the learning process and that can be adapted to the learning needs of diverse learners, across contexts, in response to different types of cognitive demands.

EXPLICIT INSTRUCTION: A MEANINGFUL ALTERNATIVE

Explicit instruction (e.i.) represents a research-based alternative to D.I. or d.i. approaches. The e.i. framework differs from these models because it is based on the teacher-effects literature as well as research in learning strategies and cognitive processes. Whereas D.I. and d.i. approaches focus on how presentation of material influences behavior, e.i. seeks to understand and capitalize on how incoming information is processed and organized by the learner. Interest in students' cognitive processes occurred as a natural outgrowth of a shift in orientation from teacher-controlled, behaviorist theories of instruction to theories of learning that attempt to teach students *how* to learn. Along with this change in emphasis, a shift occurred in the way educators viewed learners. Current theories hold that the educational process is based on building the cognitive structures of the learner's mind (Brown, 1994).

This change in approach modified our conception of the teaching and learning process in important ways. Learning is seen as an active process that occurs within the learner and that can be directly influenced by the learner. Although d.i. models (e.g., Hunter, 1982; Rosenshine, 1983) are teacher directed and share an emphasis on teaching that is structured, explicit, and clear, they emphasize the teacher's role in maximizing academic learning time. Learner-centered, inquiry-oriented approaches emphasize the learner's role in constructing learning. Since learning occurs *within* the learner, the teacher serves as a facilitator (rather than a director) of that learning. The

TABLE 1.2   Explicit Instruction (e.i.) as an Alternative

d.i.	Learner-Centered Approaches	e.i.
Teacher directed	Learner centered	Teacher structures and directs the learning process
Structured, explicit, clear	Discovery oriented	Structured, clear, explicit
Emphasizes teacher's role in maximizing academic learning time	Emphasizes learner's role in constructing learning	Emphasizes teacher's role in maximizing academic learning time *and* learner's role in actively constructing learning
	Teacher as *facilitator* or *guide*	Conceived for use in inclusive classrooms
	Tailored toward learners who are independent and self-directed	"Instruction as usual" = planning for and teaching *all* students
		Accommodations for diverse learners are integrated into the framework

e.i. framework merges these two viewpoints: the outcome of learning is not believed to depend mainly on what the teacher presents or what is going on cognitively inside the learner. Rather, the outcome of learning depends *jointly* on what information is presented and how the learner processes that information. From this perspective, e.i. is teacher led but with a greater emphasis on the ways in which students actively construct and process knowledge (see Table 1.2).

Previous approaches to d.i. were conceptualized before inclusive classrooms became widespread. Delivering whole-group and small-group instruction in an academically diverse classroom poses a particular set of challenges. As a result, teachers often continue to plan and deliver "instruction as usual." Modifications or accommodations for less capable students can become an afterthought and may include the same few options every time. These accommodations may or may not do much to help students with learning difficulties, but their teachers may not know of more meaningful ways to modify their instruction. The e.i. framework was conceptualized specifically for use in inclusive classrooms. It includes elements that have been identified by research as providing access to the general education curriculum for diverse learners, such as a high level of active engagement, use of strategies and prompts, activating background knowledge, explicit review/preview of new material and/or vocabulary, and cognitive modeling. The e.i. framework reframes "instruction as usual" as giving conscious consideration to planning for and teaching *all* students. The need for additional tacked-on accommodations can be significantly reduced because strategies that promote success among diverse learners have already been incorporated into the lesson.

Some readers may be thinking, "If components such as generating prior knowledge, thinking aloud, and formative assessment for and of learning are all components of lessons, how is e.i. different from learner-centered, constructivist approaches? Certainly, a skilled teacher can take any concept and teach it through specific steps, think-alouds, conducting an inquiry-based teaching method, and emerging student discussion." In many cases, that is true. However, it is important to consider that there are many students in general education class-rooms with highly gifted teachers who still fail to progress at the same rate as their peers. These students often continue to languish and ultimately end up in special education. Such students cannot wait for certain skills, strategies, or content to take hold incidentally. In order to accelerate their progress, structured, intentional, and sustained efforts must be made to help them achieve, including the use of e.i.

Four underlying assumptions guided the content and organization of this book. First, *the way teachers think about e.i. influences the way they teach.* Research has documented that teachers will not adopt teaching practices that do not fit with their personal beliefs about teaching and learning (Richardson, 1996). If teachers believe that e.i. is boring, rote, meaningless, and wrong, they will either dismiss it or implement it halfheartedly. Therefore, e.i. allows teachers to preserve their value for teaching that is holistic and meaningful and that promotes the active engagement of students in the learning encounter while providing the structure and control needed by many students (see Table 1.3).

Second, *a teacher's preference for certain teaching approaches should not supersede individual students' instructional needs.* It is commonly held that teachers are autonomous decision makers, capable of making well-informed instructional decisions for their students. Certainly, teachers are in the best position (as opposed to administrators, policymakers, or researchers who are far

---

TABLE 1.3   What Is Explicit Instruction (e.i.)?

e.i. shares similar goals with other approaches to teaching (e.g., constructivist, holistic, or student centered)	These goals include teaching students to enjoy and be competent at reading, writing, and math; to understand what they read and how math works; and to apply their skills in meaningful ways.
e.i. is holistic	For example, teachers can use e.i. to teach everything that is included in "literacy" (i.e., decoding, comprehension, spelling, and the writing process).
e.i. integrates smaller learning units into meaningful wholes	e.i. does not teach basic skills in isolation from meaningful contexts.
e.i. is developmentally appropriate	Instruction is tailored specifically to students' learning and attentional needs.
e.i. is not skill and drill	e.i. is skill based, but students are *active* participants in the learning process.
e.i. is not rote	The teacher constantly monitors understanding to make sure students are deriving meaning from instruction.
e.i. is not basic skills only	e.i. is used in diverse contexts and curricular areas.
e.i. is not boring and alienating	Students like it because they are *learning*!
e.i. is not all teacher directed	Students are cognitively engaged throughout the learning encounter. They have opportunities throughout the lesson to self-monitor and direct their own learning and participation.

removed from the classroom context) to know what their students need. It is important to acknowledge, however, that there are times when we hold fast to our instructional preferences out of anxiety, fear of change, lack of expertise, or entrenched ideological beliefs. A goal of this book is to challenge teachers who have rejected e.i. in the past to expand their instructional repertoires to meet the needs of *all* students.

Similarly, a third guiding assumption is that *teaching is student centered to the extent that it meets each student's instructional needs.* Definitions of student-centered teaching typically hinge "student centeredness" on the extent to which learning is directed by students. However, student-centered teaching that fails to produce learning in many students cannot be considered effective. This book conceptualizes student centeredness as providing the kind of instruction most likely to maximize individual students' learning.

Finally, *e.i. is flexible and purposeful.* Here, the word *explicit* refers to the careful structuring of the learning *process* by the teacher (see Table 1.4). The e.i. framework combines elements drawn from behavioral theory (e.g., gaining students' attention, explicit modeling, guided practice, and checking students' understanding). Also included are elements gleaned from cognitive-behavioral and constructivist theories of learning (e.g., informing students of the learning objective, activating prior knowledge, preteaching key vocabulary, and think-aloud).

TABLE 1.4   What Is Explicit in Explicit Instruction (e.i.)?

What Is Explicit?	Why?
The teacher knows precisely what she wants students to learn (be able to do) at the end of the lesson.	Unclear learning objectives result in vague teaching and learning.
The teacher tells students what they will be learning.	Students are given a sense of predictability and control. They are joined with the teacher in the instructional encounter.
The teacher focuses her attention and students' attention on the task at hand.	Students know where to direct their attention so that learning is maximized.
The teacher explains, models, gives examples and nonexamples, restates when necessary, and helps students to state and restate goals and strategies.	Knowledge that is usually covert is made overt and explicit; students are "let in" on the secret of how independent learners learn.
The curriculum is arranged so that students are taught prerequisite skills ahead of time.	Students are set up for success!
The learning is meaningful and purposeful.	Students are not taught useless facts and concepts; what students are taught now they use now and in the future; explicit connections are made between prior and current learning.
The instructional transaction follows a structured framework.	The e.i. framework combines elements that maximize achievement for many students.
The teacher provides corrective feedback.	Particularly in the acquisition stage, the teacher corrects *all* errors. Otherwise, students will practice errors and have difficulty learning more complex skills later on.

As such, e.i. is a flexible, multidimensional model. Student achievement is increased when instructional decisions are made on the basis of sound pedagogical theory and appropriate understanding of students and the learning context. The components contained in this book constitute a pharmacy of alternatives from which you can create an effective e.i. prescription for your students. As you learn these components, you will see that the decision to include *every* one of them in *every* lesson may not be instructionally sound. The use of an effective preinstructional set, for example, may serve the dual purpose of organizing student learning *and* reviewing prerequisite skills. You can manipulate the components of e.i. to form highly behavioral, tightly controlled lessons when necessary; e.i. components can also be combined with other approaches (e.g., peer learning strategies) to craft lessons that are well structured but partly student directed. Knowing these components, having categories and labels for the instructional decisions you make, knowing the research that supports them, and deliberately and expertly combining them to meet students' instructional needs are the hallmarks of the master teacher.

PLAN OF THE BOOK

This book is intended to speak to teachers about the necessity of becoming effective explicit instructors while explaining the e.i. framework in a clear, user-friendly manner. Although the theoretical underpinnings of e.i. are presented, the primary focus is on the "how" of becoming an effective instructor. Readers will be able to gain expertise a by mastering small chunks of the e.i. framework at a time—mirroring the process of teaching young students to master new skills and strategies.

Explicit instruction focuses first on getting ready to use e.i. The first order of business is to understand who exactly needs e.i. In order to avoid the mistakes of the past, e.i. must be used for appropriate purposes and in response to identified student needs. Following this discussion, we then move on to describe variables that overarch and interact with the teacher's ability to implement e.i. *Teacher presentation variables* have been identified as fundamental behaviors for communicating effectively with all students and promoting student achievement (Mastropieri & Scruggs, 1997). These variables are viewed as necessary to any teacher presentation *regardless of the model of instruction being implemented.* An explanation of three key teacher presentation variables is included in Chapter 3: teacher clarity, enthusiasm, and appropriate rate of presentation.

Another key consideration in the effectiveness of an e.i. lesson is the incorporation of *student engagement variables.* These are strategies that have been identified by cognitive research as promoting students' ability to acquire new skills and strategies through more effective storage, retrieval, and generalization (King, 1990; Pressley et al., 1995; Scardamalia & Bereiter, 1985). Strategies that actively engage students in the construction of their own learning are a distinguishing feature of high-quality e.i. Therefore, a discussion of student engagement variables is presented in Chapter 4.

Chapters 5 through 8 present the components of the e.i. framework (see Figure 1.1). Three components of an e.i. lesson—(a) preinstructional set, (b) preparing the knowledge base for instruction, and (c) instruction—have been broken down into smaller, more digestible "chunks." For example, preinstructional set has been organized into three discrete teaching skills: (a) gain students' attention, (b) inform students of the learning objectives, and (c) use informed instruction. Taken together, these three bite-size chunks constitute the skills teachers need to implement an effective preinstructional set. Although the components of e.i.

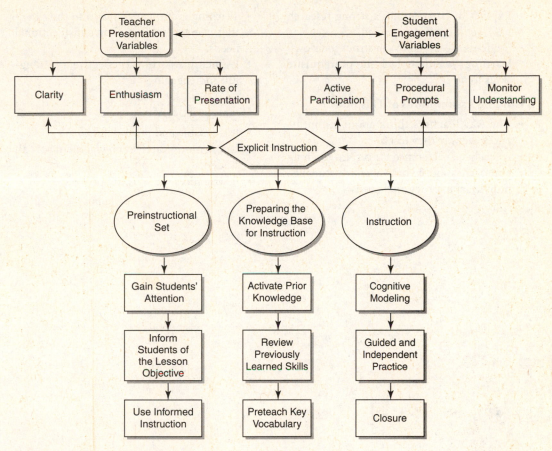

FIGURE 1.1   The e.i. Framework.

have been broken down to promote mastery of the lesson format, they are intended to be combined into seamless, smoothly paced lessons.

The final section of this book provides specific examples of how e.i. can be applied across the curriculum. Research findings regarding the effectiveness of e.i. in specific curricular areas are provided, along with lesson examples that will help you visualize what e.i. looks like in practice.

Summary

In this chapter, we examined the background and research related to e.i. As noted previously, the principles of e.i. were gleaned from the teacher-effects research as well as research on learning strategies and students' cognitive processes. Contradictions of e.i. were explained, guiding assumptions of this book

were described, and characteristics of e.i. were presented.

Contradictions of e.i.

• Many students across educational settings need e.i., but many teachers are reluctant to deliver it.

- Explicit instruction has a strong research base, yet it is often degraded.
- Students are urged to construct their own learning, yet many lack the prerequisite skills to do so.

Guiding Assumptions of This Book

- The way teachers think about e.i. influences the way they teach.
- A teacher's preference for certain teaching approaches should not supersede students' individual instructional needs.

- Teaching is student centered to the extent that it meets each student's instructional needs.
- Explicit instruction is effective, meaningful, and engaging.

Characteristics of e.i.

- It is flexible and purposeful.
- It promotes active engagement of all students.
- It structures the learning process.

CHAPTER 2

Who Needs Explicit Instruction?

Debate has raged for decades about precisely who needs explicit instruction (e.i.). Depending on who is answering the question, the answer varies widely from *no one* to *students with severe disabilities only* to *a select few students in special education* to *everyone.* The reality is that there are many students in our schools in both general and special education who need at least some e.i. Many of these students fail to acquire basic skills and strategies and continue to have difficulty reading, writing, or working with numbers throughout their school years.

Most frequently, discussions of basic skills center on literacy learning. In literacy, for example, basic skills consist of five "big ideas" that include (a) phonemic awareness—the ability to hear and manipulate sounds in words; (b) phonics—the ability to associate sounds with letters and to use these sounds to form words; (c) fluency—effortless, automatic reading of connected text; (d) vocabulary—the ability to understand (receptive) and use (expressive) words to acquire and convey meaning; and (e) comprehension—the cognitive processes involved in the intentional effort by a reader to gain meaning from text (National Reading Panel, 2000; for a list of basic skills in reading, writing, and mathematics, see Table 2.1). Research has documented the difficulties many students have acquiring basic reading skills (e.g., Catts, Gillispie, Leonard, Kail, & Miller, 2002; Shankweiler, Lundquist, Katz, & Steubing, 1999; Wagner & Torgesen, 1987). National longitudinal studies indicate that more than 17.5% of American students (about 10 million students) will experience reading problems in the first 3 years of school (National Reading Panel, 2000). Many of these students' reading problems will persist beyond the elementary grades; approximately 75% of students identified with reading problems in third grade are still reading disabled at the end of ninth grade (Francis et al., 1996; Shaywitz, Escobar, Shaywitz, Fletcher, & Makuch, 1992). Problems are particularly acute for low-income students. Students who live near or below the poverty line have lower average reading scores than their peers (National Assessment of Educational Progress, 2007).

When students experience a developmental delay in basic skills acquisition, we often assume that given sufficient time, they will catch up. However, the notion that students will catch up if given "instruction as usual" is usually mistaken; evidence indicates that this is a low-probability occurrence (Felton & Pepper, 1995). Later on, those with poorly developed basic skills are at a disadvantage in dealing with the complexities of daily life. Lack of basic literacy skills is linked with school failure, substance abuse, teen pregnancy, delinquency, unemployment, low productivity,

TABLE 2.1 Matching Assessment to Basic Skills in Reading, Writing, and Math		
Reading	**Writing**	**Math**
Fluency	Fluency	Calculation
Phonological awareness	Syntax (the way sentences and phrases are put together)	Time
Alphabet skills		Money
Concepts of print	Vocabulary (word choice)	Fractions
Sight words	Structure (mechanics including punctuation, capitalization, and rules of grammar)	Decimals
Phonics		Geometry
Structural analysis skills		Problem solving
Vocabulary	Content (accuracy, ideas, and organization)	Interpreting and using data (graphs and statistics)
Comprehension (literal, inferential, narrative, and expository text structures)		
Assessments		
Informal Reading Inventory	Formal writing assessments:	Criterion-referenced tests (Brigance, Key Math)
Running record	Test of written language	Teacher-created CBAs
Criterion-referenced test (Brigance)	Test of written spelling	Work samples
CBA	Brigance	
CBM (DIBELS)		

and welfare dependence (Bentley & Conley, 1992; Winters, 1997). Often, we fail to appreciate that for most students, reading proficiently is not easy. It requires instruction and support that is caring, intentional, well designed, systematic, and individually tailored to students' growth and development.

Research on response to intervention models (RtI) has led to an emphasis on the use of research-based instructional strategies for all students within the general education classroom. RtI research suggests that many students who are at risk for reading failure have been the recipients of impoverished literacy instruction (Vaughn, 2003). In other words, the failure of many students to acquire basic literacy skills can be traced (at least in part) to instruction that is not research based, that is inconsistently or haphazardly provided, or that does not "fit" with students' individual learning needs. Consequently, the overidentification of students with learning disabilities is widespread (U.S. Department of Education, 2002), as is the failure of many elementary, middle, and secondary school students to read on grade level (Perie, Grigg, & Donahue, 2005).

The discussion of research-based methods has become controversial as some scholars and practitioners in the field question the research underlying such methods or protest that their preferred methods are not considered "research based." Although controversial, a benefit of the focus on research-based methods is that it emphasizes that successful teaching is not about the teacher's preferred method; it is about providing high-quality instruction that fits the needs of all students within the general education classroom. In sum, it is important that *all* teachers use a variety of sound, research-based instructional strategies in order to accelerate student progress.

UNDERSTANDING YOUR STUDENTS

Much has been written about the importance of differentiated instruction within inclusive classrooms. Frequently, the focus of discussions about differentiation is on the ways in which students will *apply* their knowledge, skills, and strategies. In other words, teachers are taught to plan for variation in the ways students will *demonstrate* learning (Tomlinson, 2004). For example, if students are learning about the life cycle of a butterfly, some students will cut out and order the stages from a predesigned worksheet, others will draw and label the stages independently, and still others might engage in an independent research project on butterfly migration. In inclusive classrooms, however, students may need different types of *instruction* at the outset of skill, strategy, or content acquisition in order to learn. Less has been written about this important distinction.

Discussions of teaching and curricula often emphasize the development of higher-order thinking skills, critical thinking, and knowledge construction. As teachers, our ultimate goal is for *all* students to engage in critical thinking and independent knowledge construction. What is often left out of such discussions is the notion that not all students *naturally* develop such skills. For some, progressing along the continuum toward independent knowledge construction requires intensive e.i. in basic skills, followed by equally intensive practice and feedback (Moats, 1999). For example, development of higher-order literacy skills (e.g., comprehension, inference, summarization, and so on) is precluded by the spiraling acquisition of basic literacy skills such as decoding, fluency, and vocabulary.

As teachers expect and plan for different levels of instruction, some scholars have recommended conceptualizing students' instructional needs on a continuum (e.g., Meichenbaum & Beimiller, 1998. An example of such a continuum is shown in Table 2.2. For a given skill, strategy, or content, (a) some students have yet to acquire basic skills, strategies, and content; (b) some students have acquired basic skills but need many more practice opportunities in order to achieve mastery; and (c) still others have achieved mastery (i.e., they are fluent and automatic, and they could teach them to others or apply them in some other meaningful way).

Let's take the example of rhyming. Rhyming is a basic phonemic awareness skill that predicts students' ability to become successful readers (Adams, 1998). Some students in your class may have never acquired rhyming skills. If you say, "Tell me the two words that rhyme: *mat,*

TABLE 2.2   The Learning and Teaching Continuum

Identified Student Learning Needs		
Acquisition: Student has failed to acquire basic skills, strategies, or content	Consolidation: Student has not mastered skills, strategies, or content to automaticity	Mastery: Student performance is fluent and automatic
Corresponding Teacher Actions		
Explicit instruction of basic skills: Teacher control of the instructional transaction is high	Scaffolded practice: Teacher control is gradually relinquished through the provision of application-based and skill-based practice	Mentoring: Teacher control is low

ball, cat," these students may stare blankly or randomly guess, "Ball and cat?" Such students may have memory difficulties that prevent them from remembering all three choices or have trouble processing the phonological aspects of language. Other students in your class may have acquired rhyming skills but need more practice in order to become fluent. These students may guess the correct rhyming words some of the time but need more intensive practice in order to perform like their same-age peers. Finally, some students identify rhyming words correctly 100% of the time. At the classroom writing center, they independently write and illustrate in order to make their own book of rhyming words.

An important part of this conceptualization is that teachers assess where their students fall on the continuum for each new skill, strategy, or content taught. In other words, students *themselves* should not be viewed as representing a point on the continuum. While it is true that some students' acquisition of basic skills and strategies may be extremely limited in many areas, conceptualizing students' instructional needs in this way is intended to help teachers differentiate their instruction, not further categorize or stigmatize students.

Once you understand your students' instructional needs, you can work to design an appropriate "fit" between those needs and the kinds of instruction you provide. As shown in Table 2.2, there is an appropriate teaching action that corresponds to each identified student need. Explicit instruction is provided when the following occur:

- The goal is teaching a well-defined body of information or skills that all students must master.
- Assessment data indicate that students have not acquired fundamental skills, strategies, and content.
- Assessment data indicate that student progress toward mastery of skills, strategies, or content needs to be accelerated.
- Inquiry-oriented or discussion-based instructional approaches have failed.

At this point, teacher control of the instructional transaction is high in order to ensure student engagement and acquisition.

Once students have acquired basic skills, strategies, or content, the teacher provides multiple opportunities for scaffolded practice in many different contexts. Much of the instructional time in schools is spent practicing and applying skills or strategies that students have already learned. Most students need both skill-based and application-based practice in order to attain mastery. Skill-based forms of practice are those typically associated with "skill-and-drill" types of activities (e.g., flash cards, games, and worksheets). Skill-based practice develops fluency or students' ability to perform a task (e.g., reading sight words, writing spelling words, and calculating math facts) automatically and correctly or *fluently*. Application-based forms of practice are those we often refer to as "authentic," "meaningful," or "real-life" tasks. For example, application-based spelling practice might involve students in writing a friendly letter to a pen pal using at least five of the week's spelling words. During consolidation, the teacher closely monitors student practice and provides corrective feedback so that students do not practice errors.

Once students have engaged in enough practice to achieve mastery, the teacher's role shifts from scaffolding to mentoring. At mastery, students are self-directed enough to apply their skills in a meaningful way with teacher guidance—either by teaching someone else (e.g., a younger peer) or planning and carrying out a culminating project of their own. In a single classroom, individual students will fall at different points on the continuum at different times. Across the continuum, the type of teaching provided is in direct response to students' identified instructional needs. But how do you really know who needs what kind of instruction?

WHAT DOES THIS STUDENT NEED? THE ROLE OF ASSESSMENT IN e.i.

The emphasis on differentiated instruction and inclusive teaching has shifted our conception from a "one-size-fits-all" view of teaching to one that asks, "What does this student need?" Explicit instruction—indeed, any instruction—is most effective when applied *in response to an identified need.* Identified learning needs are not based on teacher opinion, feeling, or observation; rather, teachers closely monitor student learning by gathering concrete assessment data. These data provide the foundation on which sound instructional decisions are made. In order to plan instruction appropriately, it is important to determine what students know and monitor what they learn. In contrast to more holistic approaches to teaching that emphasize teacher observation as a primary form of assessment, e.i. requires that teachers concretely assess student progress on an ongoing basis in order to tailor instruction appropriately.

At times, it can be difficult for teachers to distinguish between students who have not acquired basic skills and those who need more intensive practice in order to master skills they have already acquired. Students who fail to acquire basic skills suffer from a *cumulative deficit*; since basic skills build one on the next, failure to acquire one basic skill leads to the inability to acquire other skills in the sequence. Over time, this results in a cumulative deficit of necessary skills. Alternatively, some students may have made initial progress at acquiring basic skills but have failed to master those skills to automaticity. Automaticity or fluency is measured in terms of speed and accuracy. For example, when students become fluent at reading sight-word vocabulary, they are able to decode words quickly, automatically, and correctly. Students with learning disabilities, however, typically require multiple practice opportunities in order to achieve mastery.

Frequent and accurate assessment is required to distinguish between acquisition and mastery problems. This can be an important distinction because these are two different problems that call for different instructional interventions. An acquisition problem indicates that a student has not learned a particular skill (strategy, content, concept, or procedure) and must be explicitly taught. For example, a glaring indication of acquisition failure in literacy is a student, adolescent, or adult who has not learned to read. Such individuals may have insufficient knowledge of prereading skills (e.g., the ability to recognize rhyming, to segment words into their constituent sounds, or to blend separate sounds into words) and poor knowledge of phonics and/or complex phonics patterns (e.g., vowels, double vowels, complex vowel combinations, or vowel/consonant combinations). They may also have severe processing problems that impede the acquisition of certain reading skills. For example, a student with blending problems might be able to say the individual sounds in *cat*, but when asked to blend the three separate sounds, he or she would persist in saying the respective sounds of /c/-/a/-/t/ and not be able to produce the word *cat* by blending them together.

Mastery of a concept, skill, or procedure means the individual's application of it is automatized, fast, and accurate. Mastery in performance is always measured or expressed in speed of errorless performance. Mastery problems, therefore, indicate that the student has learned the concept, skill, or procedure; however, learning has not reached the point of automaticity where performance is not only accurate but also fast, smooth, and without hesitancy. Lack of mastery in reading, for example, is evidenced when a student takes a long time to say a word and manages to do so only after much subvocalizing and occasional repetition of word parts. This suggests that the student does know the specific letter–sound associations in the word but has not learned those associations well. He is unsure of the letter–sound associations in the word, thus the hesitation and need for subvocalization. If he had mastered the letter–sound associations, he would have quickly, correctly, and automatically decoded the word.

For many students, there will be certain areas in which they show acquisition problems and others in which they show mastery problems. Identifying problems in this way enables us to apply the most effective and appropriate instructional focus. For acquisition problems, early identification and intervention are required. The focus is on teaching students what they have not learned, often through e.i. Once the needed concept or skill has been learned, adequate practice is provided so that mastery can be achieved. Mastery problems require an explicit review of what has already been learned, followed by practice of the concept, skill, or procedure until mastery is clearly and definitively reached. In sum, acquisition problems require intensive e.i. from the teacher in the areas where acquisition failure has occurred. Mastery problems may require reteaching in the form of e.i., followed by explicit review and motivating forms of ongoing practice.

MONITORING STUDENT PROGRESS

An effective system for determining students' instructional needs includes multiple types of assessment that each serve different useful functions (Carr & Harris, 2001). A combination of approaches allows teachers to gain the most informative data regarding student performance. Three components that can be combined to create a comprehensive assessment program are large-scale assessment, curriculum-based assessment, and classroom assessment. Curriculum-based assessment can be used to target instruction toward the development of specific skills and strategies. This, in turn, helps inform classroom assessment across the curriculum. Classroom assessment strategies are informed by large-scale assessment data at grade level and instructional level (if they are different). Using multiple measures is ideal for ensuring the success of all students because it generates the most detailed picture of student progress. Table 2.3 presents the different forms of assessment and the questions that can be answered with their respective results.

Large-Scale Assessment

Since the implementation of No Child Left Behind (2001), the role of large-scale assessment has grown considerably. States are required to administer annual assessments to all students in reading and mathematics at grades 3 through 8 and once at grades 10 through 12 and to annually assess the English proficiency of English-language learners. One outcome of the increased emphasis on standardized testing is that it has highlighted a deep void in teachers' training in and understanding of assessment design and use (Wiggins, 1993). Teachers are now giving many more tests and assessments, but they do not always understand what to do with the results. Because large-scale assessments are tests administered to large numbers of students (e.g., those in a district or state), the results can be useful for comparing student progress to standards and/or other groups of students (Popham, 2001). Despite the increased attention paid to large-scale assessment, it is important to remember that it is only *one* part of a comprehensive assessment system.

Whereas large-scale assessment data can be used to determine whether students have mastered specific competencies and to identify broad instructional areas that need additional attention, curriculum-based assessment and classroom assessment help teachers decide what to teach and how to teach it.

Type of Assessment	What Questions Do the Results Answer?	How Often Is It Used?
TABLE 2.3 Deriving Meaning from Assessment Data		
Curriculum-based assessment	Are students making expected progress on core educational skills? In what skills does he or she need additional help?	Weekly or quarterly, depending on student progress
Classroom assessment	Are students making expected progress toward mastery of their grade or level curriculum? How well do students understand what has been taught?	Weekly or biweekly
Large-scale assessment	Does the district's curriculum meet the needs of students? How does student progress compare to state and national standards?	Annually
Alternative proficiency assessment	Are students making expected progress toward mastery of their grade or level curriculum? How well do students understand what has been taught?	Weekly or biweekly

Curriculum-Based Assessment

Curriculum-based assessment (CBA) uses CBA measures to systematically monitor progress. Although it originated as a special education tool, CBM has been applied within general education contexts to assess curriculum areas that contribute to success in school. Curriculum-based assessment has several characteristics that make it a useful tool for monitoring student progress in the classroom. There are many different models of CBA, but all are modeled on the assumption that teachers should assess what is taught (Deno, 1987). The results of CBA measures are easier to understand than normative tests because they are based on typically used classroom curriculum. CBA involves direct, repeated assessment of targeted academic areas or skills. In each area, probes are developed from the books or materials that are used in the student's classroom. Probes (e.g., brief reading passages, spelling lists, samples of math items from the curriculum) are then used to collect data on student performance in math, reading, and spelling. CBA provides a structured way to see how well a student is performing on the materials the teacher uses in class and to compare student performance to that of his or her same-grade peers. Because CBA measures are conducted routinely and often (e.g., weekly or biweekly) they are sensitive to small changes in student performance, which are important characteristics when working with students who make small learning strides that can be difficult to detect with other methods.

The most important function of CBA is to use the data to make informed instructional decisions. Once data has been collected, teachers can ask themselves questions such as the following:

- Is the student progressing?
- Is my instruction effective (or effective *enough*)?
- Do I need to change instruction?
- Is the instructional change I've made effective?

Classroom Assessment

As stated previously, CBA measures are used primarily at the elementary level to monitor student progress in key educational skills. A limitation of CBA measures is that they are pencil-and-paper tasks in reading, spelling, and math. Such data alone cannot give us a multidimensional picture of student performance across curriculum areas and settings. Either in addition to CBA (at the elementary level) or as a stand-alone set of approaches (at the middle and secondary level), most teachers have their own system for assessing their student's actual performance in the classroom. Whereas CBA provides important information to teachers about the effectiveness of their instruction for meeting students' learning needs, classroom assessment provides data about student progress in the grade-level curriculum.

Typically, classroom assessment is divided into two broad categories: formative and summative. A combination of formative and summative assessments can provide the most thorough method of classroom accountability. Formative assessments are ongoing forms of classroom assessment that teachers can use to guide their instruction and provide targeted feedback to students. In K–12 classrooms, formative assessments typically include items such as writing samples, running records, term papers, anecdotal notes, quizzes and essays, teacher-developed tests, or lab reports. If the results of a formative assessment indicate that students have not adequately grasped a concept, the teacher can devote attention to problems in a timely manner. She may decide to engage students in a focused review, modify the instructional approach, or give further corrective instruction. Formative assessment data is also valuable for students because it helps them monitor their own progress.

At the classroom level, summative assessments are used to evaluate the effectiveness of instructional programs at the end of a predetermined time period. The purpose of summative assessment (e.g., chapter tests, unit tests, midterm and final exams, culminating projects, or multimedia reports) is to make a determination about student proficiency after an instructional phase is complete. As with CBA, the ultimate purpose of classroom assessment data is to identify students who are not making expected or adequate progress. Classroom assessment is effective to the extent that teachers use this information to identify areas of additional support, targeted instruction, or changes in instructional approach.

ASSESSMENT AND e.i.: HOW DO THEY FIT TOGETHER?

As discussed previously in this book, e.i. should be applied for specific purposes, at particular times, to teach particular skills, strategies, and content. Assessment data provide an outline of what students need to learn. In combination with other information the teacher brings to bear (e.g., knowledge of the student's learning style and interests, the classroom context, available materials, and potential curriculum barriers), an appropriate decision can be made as to how to teach it. Because CBA is a tool for monitoring student progress in basic skills and *e.i.* is a method that can be used to teach basic skills, these two strategies can be used together to accelerate student progress. They can be used effectively, however, only if the teacher knows the scope and sequence of appropriate skills that must be taught in order to improve performance on the CBA probes. Classroom assessment data can be used to describe students' independent performance on a wide array of skills across the curriculum, a depiction of the types of support and level of student success when the supports are in place, and an explanation of the instructional strategies used and their efficiency. Taken together, all this information can be used to create a complete picture of students' instructional needs—including those who may need e.i.

CASE EXAMPLE: JULIA

Figure 2.1 presents a reading assessment report for a fourth-grade student named Julia. Julia's assessment report includes CBA data on six fundamental reading subskills. The bar graph in the figure relates to each subskill. Graphing the data allows Julia's teacher to easily identify subskills in which she is 1 or more years behind grade level and to prioritize these instructional areas. In addition to her CBA data, Julia's teacher also consults formative and summative classroom assessment data, such as anecdotal notes from classroom observations, journal entries, weekly spelling tests, and reading chapter tests. In essence, Julia's assessment report provides a detailed "map" for her teacher's instruction.

Although she is a fourth grader, Julia is at least two grade levels behind in several reading subskills: phonics (−2), spelling (−2.5), and reading comprehension (−2). Her CBA data show that in phonics, for example, Julia has difficulty with vowel pairs (e.g., ea, oa, ie, ai) and more complex vowel combinations (e.g., eigh, ough, igh). Her failure to master these skills is reflected in her CBA spelling score, which is several grade levels below expected for a fourth grader. Not surprisingly, her weekly spelling test scores are also low (72% and 45%). Julia scored better on assignments such as the Earth Day essay (90%) and the recycling project (100%), in which she was given the opportunity to write a rough draft and use peer editing and revision to improve her work.

These data provide important information to Julia's teacher regarding what to teach and how to teach it. Although Julia has acquired basic phonemic awareness and phonics skills, she has not attained mastery of more advanced phonetic skills. This difficulty impedes her ability to read and comprehend grade-level texts. As a result, her teacher regularly provides explicit review and practice of vowel pairs and complex vowel combinations in order to improve her decoding skills. In the past, informal review of phonics skills has failed to improve Julia's performance. Therefore, her teacher conducts explicit, daily reviews in the form of brief *e.i.* lessons. Julia then engages in brief spurts of intensive, skill-based practice throughout the day. She completes a pocket chart game, uses spelling flash cards with a peer, and engages in a SmartBoard phonics activity designed for her by the teacher. In addition, her teacher continues to provide e.i. to help Julia acquire reading comprehension and vocabulary learning strategies. Application-based practice comes in the form of daily writing assignments such as journal entries and writers' workshop.

Student: Julia S.	**Assessment Date:** 4/19/07	**Age:** 9 years, 5 months	**Grade: 4**
Reading Area		**Range**	**Julia's Score**
High frequency words: Ability to quickly identify frequently occurring words; responses are time		K–high third	mid–third
Word recognition: Ability to read leveled lists of words including phonetically irregular words		K–high 12th	high second
Word Analysis (Phonics): Knowledge of basic phonetic rules and decoding skills		K–high fourth	high second
Receptive Vocabulary (word meaning): Oral vocabulary skills measured using leveled lists of vocabulary words		K–high 12th	high fifth
Spelling: Spelling skills and exposure to grade-appropriate words		K–high 12th	high first
Reading comprehension: Ability to answer factual and inferential questions about a silently read passage		K–high 12th	high second; 33% of errors on factual questions; 66% of errors on inferential questions

Julia CBM Graph

Classroom Assessment Data							
Overall	Earth Day Essay	Recycling Project	Spelling Test 3.2	Reading Chapter 3 Test	Spelling Test 3.3	Journal	Journal
74 C	90	100	72	70	45	89	83

FIGURE 2.1   Julia's Reading Assessment Report.

In summary, Julia's teacher used a variety of assessment data to inform her use of e.i. Assessment data provide critical information about whether teachers have been successful in meeting their students' instructional needs. However, assessment data can be misleading, irrelevant, and uninformative in the absence of clearly defined learning objectives.

PLANNING FOR e.i.

One you have determined who needs *e.i.* and in what specific areas, you can begin to plan *e.i.* lessons. Lesson planning provides a map of precisely what is to be taught and how you will teach it. Typically, lesson plans include at least four specific components. First, a statement of the learning objective (i.e., what students are expected to learn) is of utmost importance because having a clear goal in mind for any lesson dictates the parts of the lesson to follow. Second, a statement about necessary materials cues the teacher as to what preparations need to be made prior to the lesson. The third and most detailed part of the lesson is the "Procedure"—a set of steps to be followed in order to help students achieve the learning objective. Finally, a statement of how student learning will be assessed is typically included.

Writing Correctly Worded Learning Objectives

It is possible to target e.i. effectively only when learning goals are clear, measurable, and observable. Likewise, it is possible to create effective assessments only when instructional outcomes have been made explicit. Effective teachers, therefore, engage in an ongoing cycle of progress monitoring, setting e.i. objectives, and providing targeted e.i. toward student achievement of those objectives. This section describes how assessment data can be used to set clear instructional objectives.

An objective is a description of what we want students to be able to do before we consider them competent. Objectives are important for several reasons. First, when clearly defined objectives are absent, there is no sound basis for the selection or design of assessment, instructional materials, content, or methods. If you don't know what you want students to learn, it is difficult to select an appropriate means to get there. Clearly defined learning objectives also provide direction for students in organizing their own learning efforts. Objectives, then, provide a basis for selection and design of e.i., for evaluation or assessment, and for organizing students' own efforts at accomplishing the learning objectives.

Here is an example of how unclear objectives can hinder students' efforts to achieve the learning objective. Ms. K, a first-grade teacher, taught a lesson on using personal pronouns. She presented several sentences containing proper nouns in a pocket chart. For example, the first sentence read, "Sally rode her bike to school." Students were taught to replace the proper noun *Sally* with the appropriate personal pronoun selected from a list (in this case, *she*). However, when Ms. K assessed her students on their acquisition of this skill, they were required to replace the personal pronouns in the sentences with proper nouns. This procedure was the *exact opposite* of what was expected of students during the lesson. Since Ms. K was not clear about precisely what she wanted her students to learn, she expected her students to infer the opposite process by teaching them how to do it forward.

An e.i. lesson requires at least one correctly worded instructional objective. Teachers of older students may choose to focus on more than one objective in a single lesson. However, it is usually best to choose one focused objective for students in elementary settings. In addition to the stated learning objective, teachers often have in mind less central, incidental learning that they hope to accentuate in the course of a lesson. This is fine as long as it does not obfuscate the intended focus of the lesson. If highlighting incidental learning has the potential to diminish an e.i. lesson's clarity, save it for another time.

An objective describes an intended *outcome* of instruction rather than the *process* of instruction itself. Sometimes, it can be difficult for teachers to distinguish between an intended outcome or learning goal and an activity or agenda item for the lesson. Let us draw a clear distinction here before we go on. An objective is a statement describing an instructional outcome. It describes a result in the form of student competence. An instructional process or procedure is a means of achieving those results. For example, an instructional outcome might be to *correctly match 8 out of 10 words with their antonyms*. An instructional procedure might be to *play an antonym pocket chart game*. Instruction is the process; student competence is the result. Table 2.4 provides several more examples of outcome versus process so that this distinction is clear.

Correctly worded instructional objectives typically include three specific components: performance, conditions, and criterion (see Table 2.5). In order for objectives to be useful, they must convey your intended performance in the clearest, most precise way possible. The best objective statement is one that prevents as many other interpretations of your intent as possible. In other words, if you were absent and another teacher had to interpret your objective, he or she would teach students to perform in a way that is consistent with what you had in mind. The best way to avoid alternative interpretations is to use language that precludes misinterpretation.

TABLE 2.4   Distinguishing Between a Learning Objective and an Activity/Process

Objective	Activity/Process
A statement that describes an intended outcome or learning goal.	A means of achieving the intended outcome or learning goal.
Examples	
Write and illustrate each of the four stages in a monarch butterfly's life cycle.	Complete a worksheet on the life cycle of a monarch butterfly.
Correctly circle 8 out of 10 rhyming word pairs.	Play rhyming word bingo.
Name two factors that contributed to the Great Depression.	Discuss factors that contributed to the Great Depression in groups.
Write a persuasive essay about why we should preserve the health of our oceans.	Listen to a podcast about environmental toxins in the world's oceans.

TABLE 2.5   Parts of a Correctly Worded Learning Objective

Performance	What will students be able to DO by the end of the lesson? (active, measurable, and observable, *not* abstract)
Conditions	What will you GIVE or DENY in order for students to complete the performance?
Criterion	How well will students be able to do the performance? Phrased in terms of: Accuracy: %, 8 out of 10, all 20, etc. Speed: words per minute, in 30 seconds Quality: rubric

Look at Table 2.6. The terms listed in column 1 are "invisible"; in other words, they are not observable or measurable. Because they are open to many different interpretations, these terms are labeled "Ambiguous." The terms listed in column 2 specify a performance, but a behavioral statement would be needed in order to make them observable and measurable. For example, if you wanted students to "recognize invertebrates," there would be the lingering question of *how* they would do the recognizing (e.g., pointing, circling, or stating). In this case, the teacher would add a statement such as "students will recognize invertebrates by circling the correct option." The terms in column 2, therefore, are "Clear," but they are still not ideal. The terms listed in column 3 are clear, behavioral, and observable, so they have been labeled "Clearer." These are the best kinds of performance terms to use when writing objectives.

Precisely conveying your intent, then, involves specifying the performance you expect of the student. If the performance is covert, unobservable, or ambiguous, add the simplest, most direct behavior through which the performance can be shown. Even when striving to write objectives in action-oriented terms, teachers often find themselves writing objectives that describe feeling states or conditions. This is especially common in the beginning stages of teaching, when teachers feel less confident about exactly what they want students to learn. If you find yourself consistently producing objectives that describe ambiguous goals, try to define those goals in terms of the performance or performances that will represent their accomplishment. This will force you to write objectives that describe the performances you need to teach.

The second component to a correctly worded objective is a description of any conditions under which students will demonstrate their learning. A condition should improve the ability of the objective to communicate your intent; if this is not the case, do not include it. Describe only relevant or important conditions under which performance is expected to occur. Once again, it is sometimes difficult for teachers to distinguish between important conditions that should be specified and process or agenda items. For example, "Given a fifteen minute lecture and guided practice" is not a condition; "Given a list of factors leading to the Civil War" is a condition.

TABLE 2.6   Performance Terms

Ambiguous	Clear	Clearer
Know	Identify	State
Understand	Recognize	Draw
Appreciate	Solve	Write
Grasp the significance of	List	Point to
Enjoy	Recall	Circle
Believe	Add	Write the solution
Internalize	Discriminate	Underline
Value	Compare	Sort into two piles
Apply		
Develop knowledge of . . .		
Have a favorable attitude toward . . .		

Finally, it is important to describe the criterion by which students' mastery will be judged. A criterion can be phrased in a variety of different ways. Most often, the criterion is phrased in terms of accuracy (e.g., 85% or 8 out of 10), speed (e.g., words per minute), or quality (e.g., a rubric).

Lesson Planning for e.i.

Lesson planning for e.i. involves more detail than a basic four-part lesson plan, especially as you first begin to learn the components of an e.i. lesson. The reason for more extensive lesson planning is not simply that you must be prepared to implement a specific set of procedures. More importantly, you are training yourself to *think* in a very specific way about how e.i. should proceed. If you begin by planning down to the smallest detail at the outset of e.i. skill acquisition, eventually you will find yourself naturally following the e.i. framework even when you have not planned as carefully. The detailed lesson format can be viewed as a kind of prompt that helps you internalize the e.i. framework. As you gain independence, the prompt can gradually be withdrawn. The detailed lesson plan format for e.i. is included in Appendix A.

A checklist is included in Appendix C to help you self-check your progress as you gain competence with the e.i. framework. The checklist can also be used as a peer coaching tool. Peers can review one another's lesson plans and observe one another's implementation of e.i. and provide formative feedback.

Once you have internalized the e.i. framework, it is still necessary to write clear, complete lesson plans. Included in Appendix B is an example of block plans from a typical teacher's lesson plan book. Although these plans are brief, the learning objective (Obj.), procedure (Pro), materials (Ma), and evaluation (Ev) are clearly explicated. At a minimum, these four components of e.i. should always be carefully planned.

Summary

In this chapter, we examined the importance of ongoing assessment for guiding e.i. practice. We argued that effective use of e.i. requires an understanding of students' individual learning needs. One way of conceptualizing students' instructional needs is on a continuum, with e.i. applied to those who have failed to acquire key educational skills, strategies, or content. This conceptualization is best guided by thorough and detailed assessment data. Teachers can combine assessment approaches to gain the most accurate picture of student progress. Assessment data can then be used to create appropriate learning objectives for students.

Objectives play a key role in lesson planning for e.i., an important tool in the design, implementation, and evaluation of e.i.

When Is e.i. Appropriate?
- When the goal is teaching a well-defined body of information or skills that all students must master
- When assessment data indicate that students have not acquired fundamental skills, strategies, and content
- When assessment data indicate that student progress toward mastery of skills, strategies, or content needs to be accelerated
- When inquiry-oriented or discussion-based instructional approaches have failed

CHAPTER 3

The Engaging Teacher: Dispelling the Boring Myth

Most veteran teachers will tell you that teaching is, at least in part, a performance. After all, few other professions (other than acting itself) require an individual to be "on" for so many hours of the day. We have all had the experience of sitting in a classroom in which the teacher was less than entertaining. Although he or she may have been an expert in their content area, their bland delivery meant that the urge to sleep often overpowered our will to learn. Hopefully, we have also had the experience of sitting in front of a teacher who was captivating, funny, and a born storyteller. That teacher could have been reading us her grocery list, but we could not look away.

The most effective teachers are those who can combine their expertise in learning and teaching with a riveting performance. Learning to teach can be likened to a jazz conservatory where aspiring musicians practice scales and play exercises to hone their technical chops. Learning to play jazz involves deep discipline and the study of classical technique: mastering everything "inside the box" before artfully stepping outside it. The science of explicit instruction (e.i.) involves the events of instruction and strategies for engaging the learner. The art comes into play in how the lesson is delivered. Ask any experienced teacher, and she will tell you what it feels like when she is at the top of her game. It's the same feeling a musician gets after a great performance or an athlete has after winning a race; you know when you've delivered a brilliant lesson and your students "got it." Effective e.i. involves implementing a scientific understanding of teaching and learning in the most creative and inspiring way possible.

DISPELLING THE BORING MYTH

As previously discussed, teacher-led instruction has fallen prey to negative associations. As a result, teachers often resist engaging in e.i. out of fear that their students will be bored or that they themselves will be labeled *boring*. However, you might consider the notion that teaching methods are not inherently boring; only teachers are. One of the goals of this book is to challenge teachers' conceptions about what it means to be an effective instructor. If teachers have formed a negative association with a particular teaching method (e.g., that it is undesirable, frowned on, or even harmful), it is highly unlikely that even when called on to do so, they will do an effective job of delivering that instruction. In their heads, they may be saying things to themselves like, "This is taking too long! I'm talking too much! I need to hurry up and get through this!" If a teacher's primary goal in delivering e.i. is that it be *brief*, what are the chances that his or her instruction is going to be *effective* for students?

Instead, teachers should be concerned with delivering clear, dynamic instruction that is appropriate to their students' needs, no matter what the format. Of course, teaching does not always have to be a grand performance. At times, it can be understated—as with small groups or individuals—and still be highly effective. The purpose of this chapter is to describe teacher presentation variables that can be stage-managed to make e.i. lessons more dynamic and engaging.

TEACHER PRESENTATION VARIABLES

Teacher presentation variables describe how you can best interact and communicate with students (Mastropieri & Scruggs, 1997). Although researchers have described these variables primarily in the context of teacher-led models of instruction, effective teacher presentation skills are critical for *any* model of instruction. They take on increased importance in inclusive settings, where students with learning difficulties may vary in their ability to comprehend spoken language and/or their level of interest and motivation. A teaching style that incorporates teacher presentation variables can provide the necessary excitement and encouragement to motivate such students to succeed (Brigham, Scruggs, & Mastropieri, 1992). More effective communication with all students in the classroom can be fostered through consideration of these three variables: clarity, enthusiasm, and appropriate rate of presentation.

Researchers (Brigham, Scruggs, & Mastropieri, 1992) have described teacher presentation variables as "alterable" because they include things that teachers can alter in themselves to become more effective, as opposed to static, "nonalterable" variables, such as age or gender. Such descriptions underscore the fact that clarity, enthusiasm, and appropriate rate are things that teachers *do*, not things that teachers *are*.

It is important to note the interrelationship of the teacher presentation variables outlined here (see Figure 3.1). Both rate of presentation and teacher enthusiasm are integrally related to teacher clarity. For example, if the rate of presentation is too rapid for the teacher to be understood or if the teacher's efforts at enthusiasm cloud the instructional objective, clarity is undermined. Overall, it is important to remember that these techniques should *support* and *enhance* the pursuit of instructional objectives.

Teacher Clarity

The teacher effectiveness literature of the 1980s identified teacher clarity as a crucial communication variable (Brophy & Good, 1986; Smith & Land, 1981). As such, it is worthy of renewed attention given the prevalence of inclusive classrooms, where students may be present who have difficulty comprehending spoken language or who may not be native English speakers. A teacher demonstrates clarity when she or he speaks clearly and directly to the point of the objective, avoids unclear or vague language or terminology, and provides concrete, explicit examples of the content being covered (Mastropieri & Scruggs, 2000). As discussed in the previous chapter, learning objectives are closely linked to teacher clarity. Clear presentations focus on one objective at a time and are explicitly directed toward the

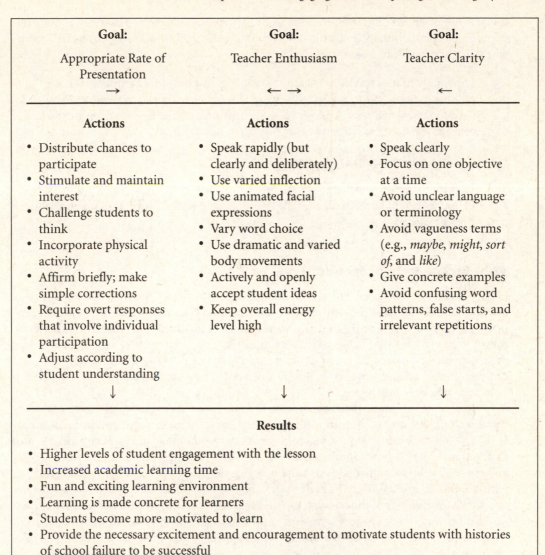

Goal: Appropriate Rate of Presentation →	**Goal:** Teacher Enthusiasm ← →	**Goal:** Teacher Clarity ←
Actions	**Actions**	**Actions**
• Distribute chances to participate • Stimulate and maintain interest • Challenge students to think • Incorporate physical activity • Affirm briefly; make simple corrections • Require overt responses that involve individual participation • Adjust according to student understanding	• Speak rapidly (but clearly and deliberately) • Use varied inflection • Use animated facial expressions • Vary word choice • Use dramatic and varied body movements • Actively and openly accept student ideas • Keep overall energy level high	• Speak clearly • Focus on one objective at a time • Avoid unclear language or terminology • Avoid vagueness terms (e.g., *maybe*, *might*, *sort of*, and *like*) • Give concrete examples • Avoid confusing word patterns, false starts, and irrelevant repetitions
↓	↓	↓

Results

- Higher levels of student engagement with the lesson
- Increased academic learning time
- Fun and exciting learning environment
- Learning is made concrete for learners
- Students become more motivated to learn
- Provide the necessary excitement and encouragement to motivate students with histories of school failure to be successful

FIGURE 3.1   Interaction Frame: Teacher Presentation Variables.

learning objective. Extraneous information that is not central to the learning objective is eliminated, and needless digressions are avoided.

To teach with clarity, it is important to eliminate vagueness from presentations (Brophy & Good, 1986). When vague terms (e.g., *might*, *some*, *usually*, *maybe*, or *probably*) are included in teacher presentations, student achievement is decreased (Smith & Land, 1981). Here is an example:

> This mathematics lesson *might* enable you to understand a *little more* about *some things* we *usually* call number patterns. *Maybe* before we get to *sort of* the main idea of the lesson, you should review a *few* prerequisite concepts.

It is also important to eliminate confusing word patterns, false starts, and unnecessary or irrelevant repetition. For example, Smith (1985) found lower student achievement in classrooms where teachers said "uh" frequently:

> This mathematics lesson *will enab* . . . will get you to understand *number, uh,* number patterns. Before we get to the main idea of the, main idea of the lesson, you need to review *four cond* . . . four prerequisite concepts. The first *idea, I mean, uh,* concept you need to review is positive integers.

Here is a comparative example of teacher clarity:

> This math lesson will help you to understand more about number patterns. Before we get to the main focus of the lesson, we will review four things that we've already learned.

Appropriate Rate of Presentation

Highly effective teachers deliver instruction at an appropriate rate. Teachers often mistakenly believe that in order to be *clear*, their instruction must be *slow*. This is a common misconception, especially when there are students with disabilities included in a group. In fact, a brisk rate of presentation throughout the lesson and a brisk rate of interaction with students keeps the lesson interesting and motivating (Mastropieri & Scruggs, 2000). An excessively rapid rate of presentation, on the other hand, may not be related to increased learning when learning outcomes are not being met.

Rate of presentation, therefore, is governed and balanced by students' degree of understanding. Often, I ask teachers to identify an appropriate rate of presentation for students with learning disabilities. Almost unanimously, they respond that such students need a *slow* instructional pace. A common concern about inclusive teaching is that the students with disabilities will hold back the other students in a general education classroom. Since students with disabilities are less likely to understand, instruction must proceed at a restricted rate. While it is certainly true that students with disabilities (or any students) profit from *clear* instruction, it need not be excessively slow. If instruction is targeted toward students' instructional level (rather than their frustration level), they will be able to keep up with a brisk pace of instruction and interaction. It is the strategies teachers use to facilitate understanding that promote student learning. A teacher who delivers unclear instruction *very slowly* is not doing her students any favors. Appropriate rate, then, is closely tied to effective assessment. It is important to determine students' instructional level so that they can derive the most benefit from your instruction.

Thus, pacing a lesson appropriately can pose a formidable challenge, especially to beginning teachers. It involves balancing many seemingly irreconcilable forces: learning to respond to each student's learning needs while maintaining the attention and interest of the group, distributing participation widely without dampening the enthusiasm of those who are eager to participate, assessing students' understanding, and allowing them to contribute to the interaction while keeping the lesson on course. These problems can be particularly acute in inclusive settings, where the teacher must attempt to adjust the pace of instruction to accommodate a range of diverse learning needs. While some students will master new content very quickly, other students will require substantially more instructional time to master the same content.

Lessons are less likely to be slowed down if the teacher has established a set of verbal or nonverbal signals that communicate important information about expected behavior to students, such as when they are to raise their hands, when they are to respond chorally, and so on. Without clear signals, students are likely to call out when the teacher wants them to raise hands or engage in other undesired behavior. Similarly, lessons become sluggish because of ambiguity in the teacher's questions or presentation. If students are clear as to what information they are expected to deliver, it is easier for them to respond.

The elements of e.i. are meant to be combined to create fluid, seamless lessons of appropriate length. A common mistake when teachers begin to implement e.i. is that their lessons drag on for protracted periods of time. Teachers should target an appropriate time period that is consistent with students' attentional skills and developmental stage. For example, 5 or 10 minutes is probably long enough to expect very young students to attend to an e.i. lesson. In elementary school, teachers might set a target of 15 to 20 minutes *maximum*. It is natural and predictable that things will often take longer than we expect. However, it is important to resist the urge to pack your lessons with every activity you can think of related to the topic. As you become more experienced with e.i., you will become adept at streamlining and pacing your lessons appropriately.

Strategies for meeting pacing challenges:

- Distribute chances to participate
- Provide think time without losing the pace
- Stimulate and maintain interest—inject mystery, suspense, humor, and novelty
- Challenge students to think
- Streamline: include only what will most effectively convey your intent; save those other fun activities for practice opportunities later
- Incorporate physical activity
- Provide feedback—affirm briefly, make simple corrections, prompt, or backtrack to a simpler question without belaboring the issue
- Require overt responses that involve individual participation, such as having students hold up fingers or response cards, physically display answers using manipulatives or whiteboards, or respond in chorus

Teacher Enthusiasm

Students are likely to learn more and appreciate the content more when teachers display enthusiasm in their teaching. Enthusiasm creates higher levels of student engagement with the lesson, thereby increasing academic learning time (Bettencourt, Gillett, Gall, & Hull, 1983; Brigham, Scruggs, & Mastropieri, 1992). Enthusiastic teaching can be particularly meaningful for students who have histories of school failure and are poorly motivated to succeed academically. Some students with learning difficulties, for example, are accustomed to performing poorly in classes and have little motivation to attempt to succeed. An enthusiastic teaching style can provide the necessary excitement and encouragement to motivate such students to attempt to be successful.

It is important to keep in mind that enthusiasm can be overdone. An essential element of enthusiasm is that it be genuine. If students view teachers' enthusiasm as sincere, they will probably welcome and enjoy very high levels of enthusiasm. If the enthusiasm seems forced or insincere, however, students will be less likely to appreciate it.

Enthusiastic teachers motivate their students to learn by doing the following:

- Creating fun and exciting learning environments
- Presenting challenges
- Fostering curiosity
- Encouraging thinking
- Making learning meaningful and concrete for learners
- Modeling interest in the subject being learned and the amount of enjoyment that can be achieved when learning occurs

Examples of teacher enthusiasm variables:

- Rapid (but not too rapid) speaking rate, varied inflection, and uplifting vocal delivery
- Physical gestures that emphasize what is being said and provide cues for when to pay particular attention
- Dramatic and varied body movements that attract student attention
- Emotive, animated facial expressions that model a state of alertness and interest
- Varied choice of words that prevents dialogue from sounding boring and predictable
- Active and open acceptance of ideas or suggestions made by students that conveys that teachers are secure with their own knowledge and anxious to hear other ideas
- General demonstration of a high energy level—enthusiasm conveyed through the teacher's overall manner

CASE EXAMPLE: MELINDA

A beginning first-grade teacher named Melinda called her students to the carpet for an introductory math lesson on coins and their values. First, Melinda read a story called *Alexander, Who Use to Be Rich Last Sunday* by Viorst (1987). Although the theme of the story related to money, it was long; students had been sitting for 10 minutes by the time Melinda finished reading. Next, she asked students what it means to be rich. A few students volunteered examples of what they would buy if they were rich (e.g., an iPod, a sports car, or a new house). Melinda reacted enthusiastically to their wishes. Then students watched as Melinda filled in an extensive graphic organizer about characteristics of different coins. By the time students were released from the carpet to engage in independent practice, they had been sitting for more than 40 minutes. At their seats, students colored and cut out coins from a worksheet. They then glued them on a graphic organizer under columns labeled with each coin name and value. Students needed a lot of assistance during seat work because their graphic organizers were different than the one Melinda had modeled. In total, Melinda's math lesson went on for an hour and a half.

Explicit instruction is meant to be clear, briskly paced, and streamlined. This example illustrates how teacher decisions about how to achieve the learning objective can affect the clarity and pacing of a e.i. lesson. As stated in the previous chapter, every event of instruction in an e.i. lesson should contribute directly to the learning objective; otherwise, it should not be included. When reflecting on her lesson, I challenged Melinda to consider whether reading the story and engaging in the discussion about what it means to be rich really contributed to her students' achievement of the learning objective, which was to be able to identify coins and their values. Melinda felt it was important to include the story and the discussion because it made using e.i. more "acceptable." Her belief was that if children's literature is included and students are asked their opinions, it makes the lesson more student centered. When asked why she gave students a different graphic organizer than the one she had modeled, Melinda said it would have been unfair if they had the same one because they could just copy from hers.

Inclusion of particular elements in a lesson does not make it inherently student centered. In this case, it could be argued that including the story and the discussion actually did Melinda's students a disservice by extending the length and pace of the lesson and taking them in a totally different direction than what she had intended. Her intent was that students learn coin names and their values, not muse about what it might be like to be rich. Rather than introducing and building toward this goal with each subsequent lesson event, Melinda led students down a mental path in which they were now focused on what fantasy items they could buy with their millions. Melinda's enthusiastic response to their ideas probably led some students to believe that this was the most important part of the lesson. Whereas some students will adeptly switch gears back to the intended focus of the lesson, others will not. Developing students' conceptions of wealth may be a valuable activity when there is extended time for discussion-based exposition of students' ideas, not as part of an e.i. lesson on coins and their values. When her lesson had already gone on for more than 40 minutes, Melinda then asked students to return to their seats to spend time cutting, coloring, and gluing. Although these are fun and age-appropriate activities at times, were they the best use of Melinda's instructional time in this math lesson? Melinda claimed to be concerned with the student centeredness of her teaching, yet she unwittingly put her students at a significant disadvantage by requiring them to complete a task she had not modeled. Their level of frustration with the task added undue time to an already overlong lesson.

This example illustrates how Melinda's instructional decisions strongly impacted the pace of her lesson and created a lack of clarity in her presentation. Although she attempted to show enthusiasm, it was not entirely useful in this situation because it had little meaningful relation to the learning objective; enthusiasm for an unclear lesson does not make it any clearer. This example also illustrates how teacher presentation variables interact. For these young students, the longer the lesson went on without a clearly defined focus, the less clear and more frustrating it became.

These may seem like trivial issues. If teachers believe strongly in the use of children's literature across the curriculum or in the fine motor benefits of cutting, is there really any harm in including these activities? The point is not that it is *never* appropriate to include these activities in your teaching. The point is to consider the impact of the clarity, rate, and enthusiasm of your presentation on students' ability to achieve the learning objective during e.i. Most teachers make instructional mistakes despite the best of intentions. Like Melinda, they may have inaccurate beliefs about what actually constitutes an effective e.i. lesson. Here are some important points to remember about teacher presentation variables:

- The clearest e.i. lessons are those in which each subsequent element of the lesson builds toward the ultimate achievement of the learning objective. If an element has the potential to obscure the objective, leave it for another time.
- Strive for clarity combined with a developmentally appropriate rate of presentation.

- Understand that enthusiasm cannot compensate for ineffective teaching.
- Rate of presentation is governed by degree of student understanding; assess and monitor student understanding to adjust the rate accordingly.

Summary

In this chapter, we discussed three teacher presentation variables: clarity, rate, and enthusiasm. These variables were framed as aspects of e.i. that can be powerfully controlled in order to stimulate student interest and engagement and to promote student achievement of learning objectives.

CHAPTER 4

The Active Learner: Dispelling the Passive Myth

Previous models of explicit instruction (e.i.) focused primarily on the teacher's behavior during instruction. Although the elements of instruction used and the way in which they are presented are critically important, the teacher's presentation creates only one-half of a balanced instructional encounter. Just as teachers need not deliver e.i. that is boring, students need not be passive receptors of information. If we frame e.i. as a transaction that occurs between the teacher and student(s), then both parties play an important role in creating an advantageous learning process. For teacher presentations to be effective, students must be encouraged to provide the second, complementary half of the transaction: active engagement. An optimal e.i. lesson involves an effective, dynamic teacher and an active, engaged learner.

If asked, we could all create a portrait of the active learner: the student who sits up, makes eye contact, and nods his or her head to indicate understanding of the topic. This student participates actively, asks questions for clarification, and strategizes effectively about how to complete tasks and assignments. Some students (typically the more capable ones) are naturally active learners; they will display these behaviors without prompting and, at times, even in response to less-than-satisfactory teaching. It may be a struggle, however, for less capable learners to become engaged and remain active during *any* kind of instruction. Therefore, it is critical that teachers routinely use variables that require all students to become actively involved with their learning. These variables take on increased significance in inclusive settings where students with learning difficulties may vary in their level of interest, confidence, and motivation.

Learning is an active process during which students create meaning by connecting new skills, strategies, and concepts to prior knowledge and ideas. Since e.i. is teacher directed, the extent to which all students actively participate depends largely on the ways in which the teacher choreographs their involvement in each lesson. Explicit instruction is an ideal time for the teacher to actively involve students and to closely monitor their understanding. It is important, therefore, that teachers help students to participate actively—to look at or handle objects, tell stories, answer questions, complete graphic organizers, refer to their own experiences, or imagine particular scenes. A key advantage of requiring active participation by all students is that misunderstandings are often revealed and can be corrected promptly.

DISPELLING THE PASSIVE MYTH

At one time or another, most teachers have been cautioned against the dangers of student passivity. All of us have heard the ugly metaphor of students as passive receptacles, waiting to be filled by a curriculum-dispensing teacher. Nonetheless, in the current environment of high-stakes testing and accountability, many teachers feel the squeeze of competing pressures: delivering the curriculum in a timely fashion versus actively involving students in the learning process. As one teacher remarked in frustration, "We are constantly told that students need to be active learners, but there are times when they need to sit and listen and I need to impart information!"

The message of this chapter is that teachers can do both. It is possible to provide e.i. *and* to actively involve students with their learning. Here is a notion to consider: students are passive *to the extent that the teacher allows their passivity*. If teachers have resigned themselves to the fact that their students will not participate, that will be the outcome. If, on the other hand, teachers create the expectation that all students will actively participate and use strategies that promote participation in every lesson, this will be the outcome. Teachers are sometimes rankled by this notion. They will say, "That's not true! I've tried everything! Some students will never participate no matter how much I try to involve them!" My response to this is usually twofold. First, you have not tried *everything*. Undoubtedly, there are strategies you have not uncovered that may work quite well. Teaching is a process of trial and error. If you continue trying and the implementation is effective, eventually you will hit on a strategy that works. Second, there are always exceptions. Classrooms are diverse and unpredictable. Individual students have particular needs and some students are more reticent than others. Nonetheless, the key is to set the expectation from the beginning that all students will participate. You will not be content to call on the same seven students time after time while everyone else sits idly staring at their hands. Clear expectations that are consistently and positively reinforced will be more successful than a "let's try this every now and then and see if it works" approach.

Teachers should be concerned, then, with incorporating elements into their instruction that require active engagement by all students. This chapter describes student engagement variables that can be used to involve students with the learning process.

WHAT IS ACTIVE ENGAGEMENT?

Early studies of student engagement focused on the time students were engaged in on-task behavior (Brophy, 1983; Fisher et al., 1980). Other definitions have since emerged that consider the more subtle cognitive, behavioral, and affective indicators of student engagement (Skinner & Belmont, 1993). Students who are actively engaged demonstrate sustained involvement in learning activities combined with a positive affect. They display behaviors such as choosing challenging activities, initiating action when given the opportunity, exerting effort and concentration, and showing enthusiasm, interest, and curiosity. Taking it a step further, active engagement has also been associated with deeper, metacognitive, and self-regulatory strategies during the learning process (Pintrich & DeGroot, 1990). According to this view, student engagement is purposeful behavior chosen by students to direct their learning process. Students engaged in simple or surface participation (e.g., answering simple recall questions) are not engaged to the same extent as those who use deeper, more elaborative strategies (e.g., paraphrasing, summarization, and compare/contrast). Use of meaningful strategies, then, is taken as the indicator of active engagement.

STUDENT ENGAGEMENT VARIABLES

A key consideration for inclusive teaching is that you cannot assume that all students have the prerequisite skills to engage on a deeper, more elaborative level. In order for all students to participate actively and meaningfully, teachers must explicitly teach and reinforce strategies that promote a deep level of cognitive engagement. In other words, active engagement is not something that all students naturally *do*; rather, it is a mental state that skillful teachers *create* in their students. Students participate actively when they do the following:

- Try to understand and make sense of new materials
- Relate ideas and information to prior knowledge and experience
- Use organizing tools (e.g., graphic organizers) or principles to integrate ideas
- Relate supporting details and evidence to conclusions
- Look for principles or patterns

The following sections discuss three student engagement variables that can be used to help all students become active and engaged during e.i.: active participation, procedural prompts, and monitoring student understanding.

Active Participation

In order to actively engage students, teachers must do more than stand up and lecture. When students are actively engaged, they focus on what is being taught and process information more meaningfully. Active engagement helps students store and retrieve information more effectively and promotes student accountability for their learning. Rather than just assuming that students who are not participating are cognitively engaged in the lesson, teachers must provide ways for students to actively and overtly demonstrate their learning by posing and answering questions, manipulating new information, and relating it to what they already know.

In most classrooms, there is a typical pattern of how student participation is distributed. During an e.i. lesson or teacher explanation, the teacher will ask a question and wait for a few students to raise their hands to respond (e.g., "Can *anyone* share an experience they've had with spiders?" or "Can *someone* summarize the paragraph we just read?"). Usually, the same students raise their hands time after time; these are typically bright, engaged learners who participate routinely. The teacher will eventually call on one of these more capable learners to answer as the rest of the students sit passively; maybe the rest of the students heard and processed the answer, maybe not.

While this pattern may be widely used and accepted, it leaves many students out of the instructional transaction. For example, when the teacher calls on a student and *then* asks a question (e.g., "*Nancy*, can you tell me the capital of Idaho?"), the rest of the students immediately know that they are unaccountable for the question and can cognitively disengage from the encounter. Even when the teacher asks a question and *then* calls on a student (e.g., "*Who* can tell me the capital of Arkansas? *Joseph*?"), the rest of the class knows they are unaccountable for providing a response. This may seem like splitting hairs; however, the ways in which teachers ask questions and promote accountability for the answers raise questions about access and accountability in inclusive classrooms: Who is responsible for posing and responding to questions? Why are some learners held accountable while others are not? Would other students be more likely to participate if given different options for participation? Are there ways of promoting active participation that do not produce undue anxiety for diverse learners?

Using an appropriate questioning technique can be particularly challenging in an inclusive setting. Managing student participation involves striking a delicate balance between keeping eager students engaged and not leaving other students behind. Occasionally, teachers will make a conscious effort to break out of their accepted routine and randomly call on students whose hands are not raised. Recently, for example, a principal commented on the "excellent" questioning technique she observed during a fourth-grade teacher's social studies lesson: "He was peppering the students with questions, rapid fire—bam! bam! bam!—very quickly, with no lag in between. He kept that lesson on track!" I asked, "What were the students doing whose hands weren't raised?" She replied, "I don't know. I wasn't focused on those students." Often, the teacher conducting the lesson isn't focused on those students either. He or she is usually preoccupied (as was this principal) with content coverage and keeping the lesson "on track."

This type of effort can be problematic, however, because when students do not know the answer or need additional think time, the pace of the lesson can be thrown off. Students may also interpret this type of random questioning as a *high-threat* instructional technique: consistently calling on students in order to "catch" them not paying attention can erode the teacher–student relationship. Implicitly, this method conveys, "I value learners who can answer my questions quickly and correctly." In fact, other students may be able to answer the question correctly if given an alternative strategy. They quickly get the message, however, that sitting passively is preferable to getting in the "line of fire."

Alternatively, teachers can create a classroom culture in which all students are involved and accountable. Particularly during e.i., it is important to involve all students. Research has shown, for example, that when students are required to give overt responses using response cards or other mechanisms for simultaneously signaling their responses, participation and learning are increased as compared to the "one student answering at a time" method (Gardner, Heward, & Grossi, 1994; Heward, 1994). Teachers, in turn, gain important data about the effectiveness of their instruction and can respond accordingly. Table 4.1 presents different types of strategies for promoting active participation and examples of each.

You will notice in the examples in Table 4.1 that some of these strategies require simple or surface-level responding (e.g., recall). Others can be used for deeper processing using higher-order thinking skills (e.g., formulating questions, making judgments, and summarizing). Teachers can use these techniques strategically, depending on the students, the topic, and the lesson context. Sometimes, for example, you are just interested in involving students in a quick review of facts or procedures. Other times, you want all students to reflect and integrate what has just been learned. Having a repertoire of strategies for active participation allows you to apply the appropriate strategy to the particular learning moment.

You will also notice that these examples involve a particular teaching vocabulary. The teacher uses words like *everyone*, *class*, and *boys and girls*. One of the best ways to integrate active participation strategies into your teaching is to consciously remove the words *who*, *anyone*, *someone*, and *anybody* from your teaching. If you are using these words, it is a signal that you are falling back on the default method of student participation (i.e., the "one student answering at a time" method). Also notice that the examples involve statements such as "This is a learning moment," "Listen and think," and "Take a moment and think." Consider how these statements

TABLE 4.1   Active Participation Strategies

Strategy	Example
Choral response	"Class, let's review the sight words we learned yesterday. As I hold up the cards, let's all read together."
Signaled response (e.g., thumbs up/thumbs down, hold up the correct number of fingers, etc.)	"Boys and girls, raise your thumbs. I will say a series of statements about spiders and insects. Thumbs up for true; thumbs down for false; thumbs sideways for not sure."
Random questioning: 1. Pose a question to the whole group 2. Provide think time for all 3. Give a time limit or allow students to signal when ready to answer 4. Randomly choose a student to respond (e.g., choose a popsicle stick)	"This is a learning moment so listen and think. [Students put their heads down and listen.] What is one reason that the first amendment is so important? When you've thought of your answer, raise your hand. [Students keep heads down and raise hands. When all students have raised hands, the teacher chooses a student at random.] Raise your heads. Jason, tell us your answer."
Written individual private response (e.g., on chalkboards, whiteboards, index cards, ticket out the door, personal digital assistants, etc.)	"Everyone, on your whiteboards, write the stages in the life cycle of a butterfly. Then hold them up so I can check."
Wireless individual private response using Turning Point student response software and wireless hardware	The teacher presents a question in PowerPoint and allows participants to submit a response by using a ResponseCard keypad; responses are sent to the computer and displayed in PowerPoint according to the instructor's preference (bar graph, pie chart, etc.).
Verbal individual private response (e.g., turn to the person next to you and whisper, classroom whip-around, think–pair–share; verbal ticket out the door, etc.)	"Everyone, take a moment and think of one question you have about how the main character changed from the beginning of the story to the end. Now turn to the person next to you and share your question. When both partners have shared, raise your hands."

differ from the rapid-fire question-and-answer technique in the previous example. These kinds of statements not only provide cues to learners about when key moments in the lesson are occurring but also signal to students that you prioritize think time and value thoughtful rather than impulsive responding. There may be times when you want students to respond quickly as a measure of student fluency (e.g., "Let's see how quickly we can read through these sight words! If you can read them quickly and correctly, I can tell that you really know them."). At such times, it is equally important to provide students with the appropriate cue.

Finally, some of the examples involve having students cover their eyes while responding. The purpose for this is twofold. First, although our goal is to promote student accountability and active participation, our intention is never to humiliate anyone. Many students who remain passive during the default method of questioning do so out of fear of being embarrassed for giving incorrect answers. Covert signaled responses (i.e., with eyes covered) allow the teacher to gauge student understanding and students to "safe face" because their peers do not see their answers. Similarly, teachers are occasionally concerned that active participation strategies promote "cheating" because less capable students can see their peers' responses. Again, teachers may want to vary students' opportunities to give covert versus overt signaled responses. For example, when a skill or topic is brand new to students, they may initially benefit from being able to see their peers' responses in order to gauge their own understanding. When the goal is to review content that students should already know, the teacher may require covert responses as a measure of individual student mastery.

In summary, when students actively participate, they are more likely to process and retain information and to engage in higher-order thinking. When teachers use strategies that promote active participation, they facilitate student learning, keep students interested and on task, foster student accountability, and make learning active and fun.

Procedural Prompts

One of the reasons some students have difficulty acquiring new knowledge and skills is that teachers do not use strategies that promote independence and transfer to other settings. Procedural prompts (or procedural facilitators; Rosenshine, Meister, & Chapman, 1996) are cues that provide students with specific step-by-step procedures or suggestions. Because they reduce the demand on working memory, prompts facilitate students' ability to use newly acquired skills or strategies independently. Students can temporarily rely on procedural prompts until they have built their own internal structures for completing the task. In other words, prompts are concrete, skill-specific references on which students can rely for support until they become independent.

Prompts are often recommended for teaching students with learning disabilities because of their utility for reducing memory demands and promoting independent strategy use (Swanson, 1999). Research indicates that procedural prompts have been used successfully to teach skills and strategies in a variety of areas, including summarization (Alverman, 1981; Bauman, 1984), writing (Englert & Raphael, 1989; Scardamalia & Bereiter, 1985), and generating questions (Billingsley & Wildman, 1984; Singer & Donlan, 1982; Wong, 1986). In a summary of research on cognitive strategy instruction by Pressley et al. (1995), strategy learning in reading, writing, math, vocabulary, and science was almost exclusively mediated through the use of prompts.

Table 4.2 presents a procedural prompt that might be provided when teaching a lesson on identifying the main idea in a paragraph (Wong, 1996). This prompt is simply a set of steps that can be written on an index card (for an individual student) or chart (for the whole class) that reminds students how to use the newly acquired skill or strategy. For any new skill or strategy taught (or a skill or strategy that students are having difficulty mastering), the teacher should consider whether a prompt might be useful.

Procedural prompts are a powerful instructional tool because simply through their use, straightforward lessons are transformed into strategy instruction. Let's consider the differences between two teachers' lessons on rounding numbers to the nearest 10. In Ms. D's lesson on rounding, she introduces the concept of rounding, explains the rules for rounding, completes multiple examples on the board, and then gives students a worksheet to complete

TABLE 4.2	**Procedural Prompt for Main Idea**

Finding the Main Idea in a Paragraph

1. The main idea sentence is the most important sentence in the paragraph. It tells you clearly about the topic in the paragraph.
2. All the other sentences in the paragraph talk about it (refer to it).
3. All the other sentences in the paragraph give you more details about it.
4. Take away the main idea sentence in the paragraph, and the paragraph won't make sense.
   a. Try it. Use this step to check if you have picked out the correct sentence as the main idea.

independently. The rounding lesson of Mr. N, her colleague, consists largely of the same elements, with one important difference: as he explains the rules for rounding, he provides students with this procedural prompt:

> *5 and above, give it a shove.*
>
> *4 and below, keep it low.*

In other words, numbers with a 5 or above in the ones column can be rounded up to the nearest 10; numbers with a 4 or below in the ones column can be rounded down to the nearest 10. Not only is this a concrete reminder of the rules for rounding, but it is also a catchy rhyme—increasing the likelihood that students will remember it after the prompt has been removed. The difference between these two lessons is that Ms. D taught rounding with the assumption that given her usual instruction, all students would be able to learn this skill. Mr. N, on the other hand, anticipated that some students would need more in order to achieve independence with this skill. Through the use of the prompt, Mr. N gave his students a useful *strategy* for remembering how to round.

The following are suggestions for using procedural prompts effectively:

- Break the task (procedure, strategy, or concept) down into manageable steps (e.g., using a task analysis).
- Provide students with a suitable procedural prompt (e.g., clearly written, large enough for students to see, etc.).
- Model appropriate use of the prompt and leave it in view for students to refer to.
- Do not abruptly remove the prompt without notifying students that you will be doing so. Instead, gradually fade students' reliance on the prompt and provide appropriate scaffolding for independent strategy use.
- Permit students to put their name on the prompt and keep it in their folder to promote student ownership and responsibility.

Monitoring Student Understanding

Throughout e.i., teacher monitoring of student understanding is critical. Monitoring understanding allows the teacher to observe students' performance to make sure they exhibit the skills necessary to complete the instructional objective. It also allows the teacher to keep student engagement high by determining if it is appropriate to proceed; if more practice or elaboration is needed; if the skill, strategy, or concept should be retaught; or if it is appropriate to abandon instruction and return to it at a later time. In addition, it serves as additional "input" for some students because corrective feedback allows them to hear information one more time or in a different way. Monitoring student understanding involves two complementary skills: checking understanding and providing corrective feedback.

Rather than viewing assessment as something that is only done at the *end*, the teacher checks understanding throughout an e.i. lesson. It is particularly critical before moving on to independent practice, during which students will need to perform with minimal, if any, teacher support. The teacher needs to check for students' possession of the necessary information to work on their own and complete the instructional objective. Many teachers make the mistake of simply asking, "Does everyone understand?" or "Are there any questions?" Students who do not understand are unlikely to identify themselves under such circumstances. In addition, the use of such a strategy does not provide the teacher with any diagnostic information regarding the learners' skills. Therefore, use of an effective strategy is essential for gauging students' understanding appropriately.

The following types of strategies can be used from the outset and repeated throughout the lesson as the teacher monitors student progress. You will notice that some of these strategies are similar to those discussed previously in the section on active participation. Indeed, some of the same strategies that maintain student engagement throughout e.i. provide important data to the teacher about how well students understand. These strategies are meant to be employed as quick and easy forms of assessment, giving the teacher a large amount of diagnostic information in the quickest possible time frame.

Examples of Strategies for Checking Student Understanding

- Sampling
    a. Pose questions to the whole group in order to focus all students on the problem and develop readiness to hear the answer
        i. "Everyone, raise your hand when you know the answer to this question."
    b. Get answers from representative members of the group (e.g. high, average, low)
- Signaled responses from each individual group member
    a. Students select answers by showing a certain number of fingers
        i. "Signal me whether you would 1) add or 2) subtract by holding up that number of fingers."
    b. Thumbs up or down for "agree" or "disagree," to the side for "not sure"
        i. "Thumbs up if the word I say has the **-at** word family, thumbs down if it doesn't, thumbs to the side if you're not sure." (signaled response)
    c. Raise hands when examples are correct
- Individual private response
    a. Written (e.g. on a slate or dry erase board, index card, PDA, etc.)
        i. "Write the names of the three important parts of a story we have discussed on your slate. Then hold it up."
    b. Whispered to the teacher so each student is accountable for demonstrating possession of, or progress toward, achievement of the required skill

c. Students whisper to one another, followed by the teacher's use of sampling
   i. "Whisper to your buddy two rhyming words. Then raise your hand and tell me."

Nonexamples of Strategies for Checking Student Understanding

- "Does everyone understand?"
- "Are there any questions?"
- "Let's move on."

An important corollary to monitoring student understanding is providing appropriate corrective feedback. Giving effective feedback requires considerable *anticipatory teaching*. This means that the teacher anticipates obstacles or barriers to a particular student's understanding and responds to the student at his or her current level of understanding. In this way, the teacher helps the student work toward a response that advances his or her understanding on the way to achieving the instructional objective. In other words, the extent to which the teacher anticipates barriers to student understanding and provides useful corrective feedback can either help or hinder a student from moving along the continuum toward independent, self-directed learning.

At times, teachers fail to respond appropriately to student answers because of inattentiveness or distraction. Beginning teachers, in particular, are often self-conscious and so focused on their own behavior during the lesson that they fail to effectively process students' responses. Failure to give appropriate corrective feedback implicitly signals students that paying attention, responding correctly, and mastering the subject are not to be taken seriously.

Table 4.3 presents examples of corrective feedback that can be given in response to particular types of student answers. When checking students' understanding, potential responses to incorrect answers include reviewing key facts or rules, reexplaining the steps needed to reach a correct solution (preferably by modeling the use of a procedural prompt), or scaffolding with clues or hints. When these types of corrective feedback are used with individual students, they also benefit others in the group by clarifying information that may have been unclear or partially learned.

TABLE 4.3 Student Answers and Corrective Feedback

Type of Answer	Teacher Response
Quick, correct answer	Move on to new question; maintain pace of lesson
Correct but hesitant	Provide brief feedback on why the answer is correct
Careless mistake; incorrect answer	Correct student error and move on to maintain pacing
Inaccurate answer due to facts or processing	Restate question in simpler form; provide clues/prompts; reteach if necessary

Summary

This chapter examined the importance of incorporating student engagement variables into e.i.. Effective use of e.i. requires creating a deep level of engagement for all students throughout the lesson, including those with diverse learning needs. Teachers can combine student engagement variables to create active participation in the learning process, to promote the use of learning strategies, and to consistently monitor student progress toward achievement of the learning objective.

This chapter concludes Part I of this book. As discussed throughout Chapters 1 through 4, e.i. draws from best practices that include strong assessment strategies; development of instructional objectives based on assessment; clear, dynamic teacher presentations; and a high level of learner engagement. This discussion sets the stage for Part II: learning the e.i. framework.

PART TWO

The Explicit Instruction Framework

CHAPTER 5

Preinstructional Set

Now that we have discussed the necessary background for implementing explicit instruction (e.i.), we move on to the nuts and bolts—the components of an e.i. lesson. In the next three chapters, individual elements of e.i. are presented. Although discussed separately, these elements are meant to be combined to form a fluid, effective e.i. lesson. For example, you might think of an e.i. lesson as a play with several acts. Each new act (lesson element) can be thought of as a specific kind of activity that takes place within the larger play. The teacher's role is to choreograph each act so that students can work successfully across the entire performance—the e.i. lesson.

In the following chapters, presentation of each e.i. element begins with a graphic organizer that lists essential characteristics of the element, examples, and nonexamples. These are intended to function as an advance organizer for each new lesson element as well as a quick-reference lesson planning tool. You can easily refer to these graphic organizers as you begin to incorporate e.i. elements into your teaching. At the top left of each graphic organizer, you will also see a clock icon. This icon indicates the amount of time that should be devoted to that particular lesson element. Keep in mind that the time indicated is a rough estimate; individual teachers will vary in the amount of time they devote to each lesson element. Beginning teachers, for example, often have difficulty keeping their lessons brief until they have had a lot of practice delivering e.i. Secondary teachers may be able to devote extended time to independent practice across several class periods. However you decide to combine these elements, the ultimate goal is to create seamless, streamlined, well-paced lessons.

This chapter presents the three e.i. elements that are combined to create an effective preinstructional set:

- Gain students' attention
- Inform students of the learning objectives
- Use informed instruction

WHAT IS PREINSTRUCTIONAL SET?

The first "act" in a successful e.i. lesson is the preinstructional set. Based on the work of Hunter (1982) and others (Ausubel, 1960; DeCecco, 1968; Gage & Berliner, 1988; Gagne, Briggs, & Wager, 1992; Gagne & Medsker, 1996), preinstructional set (sometimes called *anticipatory set*, *preset, advance organizer*, or *set induction*) is a statement that prepares students for the instruction to follow. As the name connotes, it is intended to create a mental "set" in students so that they are in a receptive frame of mind for the lesson.

Lesson introductions are among the most frequently researched teaching skills. Much of this research promotes the ability of lesson introductions to be useful in improving levels of understanding and recall, especially when students lack well-developed prior knowledge. Gage and Berliner (1988) indicated that providing an advance organizer (i.e., telling students in advance what will happen during the lesson) facilitates student comprehension and recall. Similarly, DeCecco (1968) cited the *expectancy function* of teachers: teachers are in the best position to shape student understanding and behavior when they have prepared students in advance for what is expected.

Preinstructional set serves at least four primary purposes, depending on the students, the topic, and the lesson context. First, it is intended to focus student attention on the lesson. Second, it creates a cognitive framework for organizing the skills, strategies, or concepts to follow. In this way, storage and retrieval of new information is facilitated. Third, it can extend understanding and application of new ideas. This is often accomplished through the use of examples and nonexamples. Finally, it can stimulate student interest and involvement in the lesson. Active involvement at the beginning of the lesson can increase curiosity and sustain student interest in the lesson.

In accordance with these purposes, preinstructional set consists of three discrete teaching skills: gain students' attention, inform students of the learning objective, and use informed instruction. The following sections describe each of these elements in detail.

Gain Students' Attention

An effective attention-gaining strategy is the first step to an effective e.i. lesson (see Figure 5.1). At the start, the teacher should focus students' attention. Some teachers fail to do this and purposely start the lesson in a loud voice in an effort to get students to pay attention. This type of behavior constitutes talking *at* rather than *to* students and causes many learners to miss the beginnings of lessons. Once you have begun teaching without fully gaining student attention, you have implicitly conveyed, "I don't really care if you listen to this lesson or not. What I have to say isn't that important." Once this message is conveyed, subsequent efforts to regain student attention can be difficult. Rather than launching into lessons without first gaining full attention, teachers should develop effective strategies for helping students create a mental focus on what is about to be learned.

Explicit instruction often occurs soon after a transition. Students may be physically arriving at a new spot (e.g. from desks to carpet) and in the process of mentally "shifting gears" away from the activity just concluded. Because transitions can be chaotic, gaining students' attention is crucial for eliciting attending behavior and a deliberate readiness for the content of the ensuing lesson. Obviously, if students' attention is not gained, you cannot be confident that they are focused on the learning about to take place. Therefore, teachers should establish that they expect full attention to lessons at all times.

Routines for introducing lessons tell students that the transition between activities is over and a new one is about to begin. Thus, each e.i. lesson begins with an instructional event that engages students' attention, interest, and/or curiosity. At times, this will involve stimulating students' attention from a state of total disengagement to one in which they are listening and looking attentively. Alternatively, this may involve raising their attention from an already receptive state to a higher level of curiosity, interest, and engagement.

☐ 30 seconds

Essential Characteristics

- Done at beginning of lesson.
- Focuses students' attention and interest on the learning about to take place.
- Can be a focusing statement, a standard signal, or a question that elicits curiosity.
- Brief and effective (a few seconds to 2 minutes).
- Intensity will vary with characteristics of the instructional group.

Examples	Nonexamples
• "Right now you should be sitting silently, pretzel-legged, looking at me. Great job! Let's begin our lesson."	• "Okay."
	• "Open your books to page 47."
• "Have you ever wondered why some animals come out only at night?"	• "Now we're going to do math."
	• Begin the lesson in a loud voice.
• Teach and practice a signal such as clapping a rhythm and having students respond.	

FIGURE 5.1   Gain Students' Attention.

After giving the signal or using the intended focusing strategy, the teacher should pause momentarily and allow it to take effect. Once attention has been gained, the teacher should begin briskly by describing the learning objective for the lesson. The pause between giving the signal and beginning the lesson should be brief, just long enough for students to focus their attention. If the pause is too long, students will lose the sharp focus that has been created. It is important, then, that the teacher act quickly if a few students do not respond. Facial expressions and gestures can be used to indicate that they should pay attention, or their names can be called. If this is not enough, a brief focusing statement can be added, such as, "Josh, look over here."

Characteristics of a Good Attention-Gaining Strategy

- Attention-gaining activities should be brief and effective, lasting only long enough to get students ready so that the major portion of instructional time is available for accomplishment of the learning objective.
- A standard signal that tells the group that "we are now ready to begin a lesson" is useful. However, the signal must be taught ahead of time and practiced repeatedly in different contexts to ensure that it is recognized by all students as a sign that they should attend to the teacher.
- The intensity of an attention-gaining strategy will depend on the group of students. For example, a less capable fourth-grade group that meets after lunch may require a more dramatic attention-gaining strategy than will a self-directed, eager group meeting first

thing in the morning. Familiarity with your students will help with selection of the right strategy for gaining their attention.

Examples of Attention-Gaining Strategies

- Teach and use a signal such as holding up two fingers or placing a finger over the lips to signal quiet. For signals to be successful, it is essential to use your e.i. skills to explicitly teach the signal, role play the signal repeatedly, and practice it in multiple contexts.
- Review expectations for behavior before beginning an e.i. lesson. For example,

  "At this time you should be sitting up straight, pretzel-legged, looking at me. Hands are still and in your lap. Great job! Let's begin."

  "SLANT!" (Sit up, Lean forward, Ask questions, Nod your head, Track the speaker)

- Affirm students for their good attending behavior. For example,

  "It's wonderful when I come to the carpet to begin a lesson and you are already quiet, sitting up straight, keeping your hands still in your laps, ready to listen. Terrific job! Let's begin."

- Relate the content of your lesson to students' interests or use questions to arouse their curiosity. These questions, called "openers," are not intended to have a single right answer or even to reflect the fine details of what will follow but rather are meant to *amuse*, *stimulate*, or even *bewilder* students so that they become interested and receptive to the content that follows. For example,

  "Have you ever wondered why some animals only come out at night?"

  "Can you guess what I have in this box?"

Nonexamples of Attention-Gaining Strategies

- "Okay."
- "Open your books to page 47."
- "Now we're going to do math."
- Being the lesson in a loud voice.

In order for attention-gaining strategies to be effective, they must be explicitly taught using multiple examples and nonexamples, role-played, practiced in multiple contexts, and consistently reinforced. For example, at the beginning of the school year, the teacher decides which attention-gaining signals she wants to use (e.g., hand claps and response or call-and-response). During the first few days of school, the teacher explains and explicitly models the signal for students. The teacher and students role-play responding to the signal. The teacher randomly uses the signal in multiple contexts and then positively reinforces students for responding to it.

Ideally, once students have learned the signal or focusing statement and you have positively reinforced it over time, they will respond with minimal effort on your part. For example, a few weeks into the school year, students become familiar with the routine. They know that explicit instruction takes place on the carpet at a particular time each day. You have given a signal for students to sit quietly on the carpet. When you come to the carpet and sit in the teacher's chair, students automatically give you their attention. They have internalized the focusing signal and become independent; they give you their full attention without your having to do more.

An important notion for all teachers to consider is what good attention looks like. This is significant because having criteria for acceptable attending behavior helps you know when full student attention has been gained. In addition, you can more easily convey your expectations to students when you have clearly defined them for yourself. Research in learning strategies, for example, has attempted to teach students with attention problems a metacognitive strategy for monitoring their own attending behavior. The SLANT strategy (Ellis, 1989) includes very specific criteria for giving someone your attention. The intent behind SLANT is to help students develop the same kinds of attending behavior used by independent, successful learners. If it were okay for students to lie on the floor, this strategy would look very different: lie down, look around, daydream, and think your own thoughts. Individual teachers may have different criteria for what student attention looks like. What is irritating and off limits to one teacher may not be a big deal to another. One teacher may be comfortable allowing students to lounge in beanbag chairs during e.i., while another may not. Whatever good attending behavior looks like to you, it is important to clearly convey and reinforce your expectations to students.

What can you do if your attention-gaining strategy doesn't work? Telling students to simply open their books or making a broad statement about your next activity (e.g., "Now we're going to do spelling.") are not effective strategies for gaining attention. These statements do not provide any information about the lesson to follow or its value. In fact, they implicitly convey that school is about accomplishing a series of activities rather than learning. Similarly, there is a difference between gaining student attention and maintaining it. Maintaining student interest and engagement can be difficult for some teachers to establish. Do not continue to teach if students are not paying attention.

If you consistently have difficulty gaining and/or maintaining student attention, there could be several explanations. Perhaps you have not clearly established your expectations for student attention; somehow they have gotten the idea that you are not absolutely serious about their learning. You may not have taught your expectations explicitly enough, or your implementation may not be effective. Overused, tired strategies will eventually lose their effectiveness. Even effective signals can lose their power if the teacher has not used them recently or positively reinforced students for responding. In this case, reteaching and more consistent reinforcement is necessary.

A useful way to frame student attention is as a tacit, mutual agreement: in return for their attention, you provide students with instruction that is engaging, meaningful, clear, and appropriate. Some teachers mistakenly believe that they can simply demand students' attention to meaningless lectures or tasks for inordinate lengths of time. If students refuse to give you their attention, it may be because you have violated the agreement. Therefore, it is always important to ask yourself why you have lost or failed to sustain students' attention. Is the lesson too difficult? Are students talking to each other to figure out what to do because your teaching is unclear? Have you droned on for 40 minutes when your students' attention span is only 10 minutes? If so, they are giving *you* a signal to wrap it up.

Finally, commanding student attention is a skill that new teachers often find difficult. Unresolved feelings about authority can sometimes be the cause. Most teachers want to be liked by their students. Others hold strong personal beliefs about student-centered classrooms. Fears about seeming too authoritarian or "mean" can be tied in with those beliefs. One important thing to remember is that discipline is a form of caring. It is not mean or authoritarian to teach students to attend and hold high expectations for their attending behavior. Being able to give and sustain attention and to listen and respond effectively are important life skills that will help students become successful independent learners. Failure to teach such skills would be doing students a grave disservice.

Inform Students of the Learning Objective

There are at least four kinds of information that will help prepare students for any given instructional event: learning objective, learner activities, teacher activities, and evaluation activities (see Figure 5.2). Research has commonly advised teachers to introduce lessons by stating the learning objective in language that is meaningful to students. This lets students know what to expect and helps them to prepare to learn efficiently (Ausubel, Novak, & Hanesian, 1978; Mayer, 1979).

When instructional objectives are properly phrased as intended learning outcomes (i.e., as the types of student performance we are willing to accept as evidence of learning), they serve a number of useful purposes. A clear statement of instructional objectives provides a focus that results in more effective learning and teaching. Instructional theorists have shown that goal-directed learning is central to self-regulated learning processes (Schunk, 2003). In the hands of students, objectives promote self-direction by eliminating the ambiguity and waste that come from forcing them to guess at what the important outcomes of instruction might be.

Students are much more likely to find out what they need to know if they know what they are looking for. Likewise, teachers teach more effectively when they have this same information.

☐ 30 seconds

Essential Characteristics

- Research advises teachers to introduce activities by stating the learning objective in language meaningful to students.
- Phrased in terms of what students will be able to *do* on completion of the lesson.
- Provides a focus that results in more effective, goal-directed learning and teaching.
- * Learners know what to expect.

Examples	Nonexamples
• "At the end of today's lesson, you will be able to read and spell words with the -*ell* word family."	• "Today we will study Chapter 1 and answer questions about it."
• "At the end of today's lesson, you will be able to write three detailed sentences about Martin Luther King Jr."	• "Now we are going to do social studies."
• "When we finish our lesson, you will be able to make a correct introduction of a friend to your teacher."	• "Given five single-digit math addition problems, you will be able to solve them correctly 80% of the time."
	• "I am going to go over . . ."
	• * "I will teach you . . ."

FIGURE 5.2   Inform Students of the Learning Objective.

Clearly stated instructional objectives also result in effective planning. Too often, instructional planning focuses on the methods and materials of instruction without a clear idea of how students are to demonstrate what they have learned. Appropriately phrased instructional objectives provide a basis for selecting the methods and materials of instruction that are most likely to bring about the desired learning. It is valuable to determine what kind of learning activities students will carry out, but such decisions can be made only *after* it has been determined what students will accomplish. Once learning outcomes are identified and described, activities that are appropriate for attaining those outcomes can be chosen.

Some teaching models advocate *against* informing students of the learning objective at the outset of the lesson. These models (e.g., inquiry- or discovery-oriented approaches; Bruner, 1961; Papert, 1980; Steffe & Gale, 1995) view learning as a process of independent knowledge construction by the learner or collaborative knowledge construction among small groups of learners. If the teacher dictates the objective from the outset, students are not free to make their own hypotheses or draw their own conclusions. Teachers who prefer inquiry-oriented approaches may feel conflicted about directing students toward a predetermined learning objective. However, it is important to remember that e.i., like other instructional approaches, is most effective for teaching specific kinds of skills, strategies, and content. Even when used at the appropriate time, some students will need more structure and direction than inquiry-oriented approaches typically provide in order to draw appropriate conclusions.

A distinction can be drawn between how teachers phrase instructional objectives for use in their own lesson planning and for use in informing students of the same objectives. A more formal approach is necessary for teacher planning, which includes the three key characteristics discussed in Chapter 2:

1. *Performance.* An objective always says what a learner is expected to be able to *do*. A performance must be visible, like *write*, *add*, *solve*, or *recite*. Words such as *understand*, *apply*, or *know* are open to too many interpretations to be useful in an objective.
2. *Conditions.* Wherever necessary, an objective describes the important conditions under which the performance is to occur.
3. *Criterion.* An objective describes the criterion of acceptable performance by describing how well the learner must perform in order to be considered acceptable.

Examples of Usefully Stated Instructional Objectives for Teacher Planning

- Given 10 minutes of instruction and a lab exercise, students will identify and label a plant's roots, stem, leaves, flower, and seeds. Criterion: 80%.
- Given a bar graph and a list of statements, students will correctly identify four out of five statements that are supported or unsupported by the graph.
- Given a group of 10 objects, students will select one object that represents a circle and one object that represents a square with no more than two incorrect tries.

Presenting the objective to students in the formal way described previously will not be meaningful for their purposes. In order to be effective when informing students of the learning objectives, teachers should follow the following guidelines:

- Be concrete and specific; avoid describing in general terms what the task is about.
- Phrase objectives in terms of what the students will be able to *do* when they complete the lesson.

- Rate of presentation is short and sweet. Consider stating objectives both orally and in writing and repeating them during the lesson to remind students what they are learning.
- It is the learning outcome that is *most* important, not the learning activities that lead to that outcome. For example, if a teacher says, "This week we are studying Chapter 3 and will take the chapter test at the end of the week," she is not specifying instructional objectives but merely specifying the instructional activities and materials that will be used.

Examples of Usefully Stated Student-Oriented Objectives

- Today we are going to learn to identify and label the parts of a plant.
- At the end of today's lesson, you will be able to "read" a bar graph to get information about our class.
- Today we are going to learn to pick out objects that are two different shapes: circle and square.

Nonexamples of Student-Oriented Objectives

- "Today we will study Chapter 1 and answer questions about it." (These are activities or items on your agenda, not learning objectives.)
- "Now we are going to do social studies." (This is a meaningless statement that gives students no information about what they are about to learn.)
- "Given five single-digit math addition problems, you will be able to solve them correctly 80% of the time." (This is a teacher-oriented objective.)

Use Informed Instruction

Informing students of the learning objective gives them an overall framework for the instruction to follow (see Figure 5.3). For some students, however, knowing only the expected learning outcome may not be enough information to help them get the most out of a lesson. When preparing students for instruction, it can be helpful to tell them the learning objective as well as the activities and evaluation that will be required for them to achieve the objective successfully.

Students need explicit details about the lesson. Communication that informs students *how* a skill will be taught (i.e., what activities or procedures will be involved in the lesson), *what* they will be able to do by the end of the lesson, and *why* that accomplishment is important, useful, and relevant to present and future life situations is important for both learning and motivational reasons.

The teacher has a definite role in most instructional activities. Students can benefit from knowing, from the outset of the lesson, exactly what the role of the teacher will be and exactly how much guidance can be expected. How will students know if they have accomplished an expected learning outcome? How will the teacher judge their performance of that outcome? It is also helpful for students to be alerted to potential difficulties they may encounter and informed of ways to identify, anticipate, avoid, and address these difficulties should they arise. Providing answers to these questions helps prepare students for instruction and increases the efficiency of their learning.

In order for instruction to be "informed," teachers preview the lesson by providing details and information that convey specific teacher expectations. Informed instruction is provided at the beginning of the lesson, but like the learning objective, key features of informed instruction can be repeated throughout the lesson as teachers monitor student progress.

☐ 30 seconds to 1 minute

Essential Characteristics

- Students need explicit details about the lesson.
- In addition to stating *what* the current skill/strategy is, it is important to inform students *why* it is important, *how* it is to be done, and *when* (and when not) it can be utilized.
- Meaningful to students' learning and motivation.

Examples	Nonexamples
• "Today we are going to learn . . ." • "This is important to know because . . ." • "We can use this skill when . . ." • "We will know we have learned this when . . ."	• "Today we are going to do math." • "Today we will learn to play a game. This is important to know because then I won't have to explain the rules to you next time." • Speed up and state details quickly and matter-of-factly.

FIGURE 5.3 Use Informed Instruction.

Teachers can also use this information to review before the following day's lesson or over the course of the unit.

Characteristics of Effective Informed Instruction

- Lesson details need to be communicated with the same deliberateness as the lesson content. It is common for beginning teachers to speed up and speak less distinctly when giving details about what to do, how the lesson will proceed, or when the skill can be used, and then slow down again when actually teaching the lesson. When students cannot follow your directives about how or why you want them to become engaged in the learning process, they usually will silently proceed, missing the intent of the lesson.
   a. Slow down when conveying lesson details.
   b. Divide the information into steps.
   c. Be sure each step is understood.
- Avoid overwhelming students with too much information at once.
   a. One of the most common criticisms of beginning teachers from students is that "we didn't understand what to do" (Good & Brophy, 2007). Students often won't admit that they could not follow the lesson or that it was said so quickly and matter-of-factly that they just missed it.
- Specific lesson details can be organized visually for students by posting them in sentence strips on the board or on a chart. For example,

   "Today we are going to learn . . ."
   "This is important to know because . . ."

"We can use this skill when . . ."
"We will know we have learned this when . . ."
"Sources of help available to you are . . ."

- Alert students to potential barriers they may encounter and share ways to identify, anticipate, avoid, and address these difficulties should they arise.
- Teachers can review this information over the course of the lesson or use it to review before the following day's lesson.

Nonexamples of Using Informed Instruction

- "Today we are going to do math." (Again, this is a meaningless statement that doesn't give students any meaningful details about the learning.)
- "Today we will learn to play a game. This is important to know because then I won't have to explain the rules to you next time." (Learning to play a game is not a learning objective. Saving yourself time is not a detail that holds meaning for students' learning.)
- Speed up and state details quickly and matter-of-factly. (Lesson details should be clearly stated.)

Summary

This chapter discussed the three elements of an effective preinstructional set: gain students' attention, inform students of the learning objective, and use informed instruction. Now let's put it all together. Here is an example of a preinstructional set for a secondary chemistry lesson:

The teacher gives the attention signal and waits until there is quiet. Once attention has been gained, the teacher says, "Everyone pick up the Periodic Table of Elements and raise your hand when you have found the first element on the table. At the end of today's lesson, you will be able to use the Periodic Table of Elements to identify the atomic number of an element and its symbol. This is important to know because the atomic number tells us how many protons and electrons the element has. This is also important because we use element identification when we study chemistry. You will know you have learned this when you can identify the atomic number and symbol of any element from the Periodic Table of Elements."

Review

1. Why is it important to gain students' attention before beginning a lesson?
2. What are some examples of effective attention-gaining strategies?
3. What can you do if your strategy to gain students' attention doesn't work?
4. Describe two purposes of clearly stated instructional objectives.
5. How do student-oriented objectives differ from teacher-oriented objectives?
6. What lesson details are most important for students to know?

Apply

1. Imagine that you have spent the last 15 minutes in your classroom having a snack. Students have been eating and freely chatting with one another. You have instructed them to put their snacks away, clean up their area, and come to the carpet to begin a lesson. (FYI: Joe always takes a very long time to clean up and finds straightening the Lego shelf much more interesting than coming to the carpet for your lesson.) Script the first few moments of the lesson, in which you attempt to use a focusing strategy to gain students' attention.

2. For each of the following objectives, decide whether it has a single, clear meaning by marking it with a C or an ambiguous meaning (i.e., it could mean more than one thing) by marking it with an A.

    _____ Students will know the presidents of the United States.

    _____ Students will list the presidents of the United States.

    _____ Given his picture, students will call by name each president of the United States.

3. You need to explain the use of imagery in written English to a group of sixth-grade students who have not yet been introduced to this concept. Script the explanation of lesson details you would deliver to your students. Write answers to the following four questions students need answered as they begin to learn:

    a. What do I need to know or be able to do on completion of this lesson?
    b. What do I need to do to learn that?
    c. What are you going to do to help me?
    d. How will we know when I have learned what was expected?

CHAPTER 6

Preparing the Knowledge Base for Instruction

As discussed in Chapter 1, teacher effects research studied how teachers or instructional practices affected student achievement. In contrast, research on students' cognitive processes examines how teaching or teachers influence what students think, believe, feel, say, or do that affects their achievement. Interest in students' cognitive processes has shaped our conception of the teaching and learning process in meaningful ways. For example, academic learning time has often been found to correlate with student achievement (Fisher & Berliner, 1985). The study of cognitive processes, however, would emphasize that it is the students' constructive use of that time rather than simply the time itself that affects learning and achievement. In other words, variables such as learning, memory, comprehension, learning strategies, and metacognitive processes mediate the effects of teaching on student achievement.

Explicit instruction (e.i.) proposes that the effectiveness of teaching depends partly on the teacher's presentation and partly on the learner's prior knowledge and active thought processes during learning (Anderson, Spiro, & Montague, 1984; Cook & Mayer, 1983; Weinstein & Underwood, 1985; Wittrock, 1978). This chapter presents three elements of e.i. that cognitively prepare students for instruction: activate prior knowledge, review previously learned skills, and preteach key vocabulary. After the lesson has been introduced through an effective preinstructional set, the teacher can use these elements to engage the learner and facilitate storage and retrieval of new skills, strategies, or content.

Note that you probably will *not* use all three of these strategies in a single lesson but rather choose the most effective alternative for that particular lesson. For example, activating prior knowledge is probably most useful for expanding students' knowledge of a particular content area or concept (e.g., electricity, plants, or the cardiovascular system) and can be beneficial when beginning a new unit or topic of study. Reviewing previously learned skills is most beneficial for linking component skills—skills that build one on the next (e.g., in math computation or reading); before teaching the next skill in a sequence, it is important to explicitly review what has already been learned. Preteaching key vocabulary lends itself to vocabulary instruction in content areas such as social studies, science, and English and to building fluency during literacy instruction. Choosing appropriately among these elements can help students organize and relate information to foster active and efficient cognitive connections.

ACTIVATE PRIOR KNOWLEDGE

Prior knowledge provides the storehouse of experiences that are the basis for meaningful learning (see Figure 6.1). Not surprisingly, one of the most universal findings to emerge from educational research is the marked degree to which a learner's prior knowledge of a topic facilitates future comprehension (Anderson, Corbett, Koedinger, & Pelletier, 1995; Anderson, Reder, & Simon, 1996). Learning is the result of the interaction between existing knowledge and new information gained through experience with the real world (e.g., teachers, peers, and instructional materials). Learning is not a process of passive absorption. Students come to new tasks with previous knowledge, expectations, and beliefs, out of which they integrate new information by connecting old meanings to new. It is crucial, therefore, for teachers to assess what students know and believe about a topic, skill, or strategy before it is taught. Strategic teachers emphasize conscious connections to previous and future learning.

Activating prior knowledge is one of the most widely used instructional strategies; most teachers have been taught the importance of fostering active connections between new information and students' background knowledge and experience. Despite widespread belief in the value of this instructional strategy, teachers often fail to implement it in a way that garners the most cognitive benefits for students. This is due to several issues already discussed in this book. For example, perhaps the most common prior knowledge activation strategy is to pose

---

☐ 2 to 10 minutes

Essential Characteristics

- Done before the current concept is taught.
- Facilitates comprehension and learning.
- Reveals student beliefs/knowledge.
- Teacher responds by making connections or fostering predictions.
- Facilitates comprehension and learning.

Examples	Nonexamples
• Direct questioning or paper and pencil activity.	• Ask students, "What do you already know about . . .?" but do not give students the opportunity to respond.
• Ask students, "What do you already know about . . .?"	• Access to prior knowledge after the current concept is taught.
• Make a list with a buddy.	
• K-W-L.	
• Have students interview each other.	

FIGURE 6.1 Activate Prior Knowledge.

a question to the entire group and then call on a few students to respond. This strategy is effective for the handful of students who respond; however, you cannot be assured that the rest of the group has had their prior knowledge activated. In addition, teachers will sometimes activate prior knowledge around a theme that is not central enough to the lesson content.

For example, when teaching a language arts lesson on writing similes, a teacher might activate students' prior knowledge of what clouds are like: fluffy, wispy, white, wind swept, and so on. Although the teacher's intent is to use students' descriptions as a segue to an explanation of similes (e.g., "the clouds were as fluffy as pillows"), this constitutes little more than taking students down a meandering cognitive path *away* from the core focus of the lesson. Students are now thinking about *clouds* when the true focus of the lesson is on similes. Most students will quickly regroup and follow your lesson trajectory wherever it leads; others will find it more difficult to attain the learning objective in a meaningful way.

Teachers should make it a habit to ask students to share what they already know about a given subject, skill, or strategy so that they can actively link *relevant* background knowledge with the lesson goals. This practice can also reveal certain inaccurate beliefs that may inhibit students from engaging fully in the task and lead them to quick abandonment of the task at the first sign of frustration. It is important that students' prior knowledge is activated before a new concept or skill is taught so that they can readily make connections between their background knowledge and the learning that is about to take place. This information can be obtained by means of pencil-and-paper tasks that indicate what students know and what they need to be taught. A second approach is to use direct questions. Whatever strategy is used, it should foster active participation by all students.

Characteristics of an Effective Strategy for Activating Prior Knowledge

- A strategy that fosters active participation by *all* students is ideal.
  a. Quick pencil-and-paper tasks
     i. Make a list
     ii. Fill out a questionnaire
     iii. Take a brief quiz
     iv. K-W-L
     v. Peers interview each other
  b. Brainstorming or direct questioning that gives all students the opportunity to respond (use active participation strategies)
     i. "What do we already know about . . .?"
     ii. "Have you seen something like this before? When? Please think of an example. Then raise your hand."
     iii. "Everyone, have we done this before? How is this like . . .?"
- Since students may not consciously or actively draw connections between their background knowledge and the current learning, it is vital that the teacher respond strategically to student contributions.
  a. Statements that explicitly connect students' prior knowledge to the current objective or that foster predictions about the current learning will help students to organize and integrate new information with what they already know.
- Teachers may also organize students' prior knowledge graphically by means of a chart, web, or diagram.
- Rate of presentation should be deliberate while keeping students' active participation high.

Examples of Strategies for Accessing/Activating Prior Knowledge

- Before students begin a science unit on weather, ask, "What do you already know about weather? Get together with a buddy and list three things you already know on your index card. In 5 minutes, I will call you back to the circle." After the initial brainstorm session, work with the whole group to categorize or classify information into some kind of logical visual structure (e.g., a web, chart, or semantic feature analysis).
- Before reading *The Seashore Book* by Charlotte Zolotow, ask students, "How many of you have ever been to the beach? What kinds of things did you see and do? Whisper one thing to the person next to you, then raise your hand." Fill in the "K" portion of a K-W-L chart together.
- Based on the title of a book, chapter, or unit, have students brainstorm possible words that might be encountered in the text and list them on a chart. Discuss the reasons behind certain choices that may appear strange in order to reveal covert misunderstandings.

Nonexamples of Activating Students' Prior Knowledge

- Ask students, "How many of you already know something about . . .?" but do not give students the opportunity to respond.
- Access prior knowledge of an unrelated or tangentially related topic.
- Use the "one student answers at a time" approach, then fail to draw explicit connections between students' answers and the current objective.

REVIEW PREVIOUSLY LEARNED SKILLS

You may think that beginning a lesson by reviewing or practicing previously learned, prerequisite content is a common practice. However, few teachers begin lessons in this way. This is an unfortunate fact because research has shown that teacher-led reviews are an important part of the active teaching process that is associated with strong student achievement (see Figure 6.2).

Reviews are valuable to students for several reasons. They facilitate storage of skills, strategies, and content in long-term memory and stimulate students to see relationships between their background knowledge and new information or skills. Daily review emphasizes the relationships between lessons so that students remember previous knowledge and see new knowledge as a logical extension of content already learned. It also provides students with a sense of wholeness and continuity, assuring them that what is to follow is not isolated knowledge unrelated to past lessons. This is especially important for gaining the attention and engagement of less capable learners who may lack appropriate levels of relevant prior knowledge or who may be anxious about having to master yet another piece of unfamiliar content. Review and practice at the beginning of a lesson is also the most efficient way of finding out if your students have relevant prior knowledge sufficient to begin a new lesson. If not, the relevant background knowledge can be explicitly taught (or retaught).

After conducting the preinstructional set, the teacher can provide a brief review or practice of previously achieved, related learning (i.e., review the main points of yesterday's lesson that will be extended today). In this way, the teacher can be sure that students have mastered prerequisite skills and link information that is already in their minds to the information you are about to present. Daily review and practice at the beginning of a lesson is easy to accomplish. If today's lesson is a continuation of yesterday's lesson, then the review may just remind

---

☐ 2 to 10 minutes

Essential Characteristics

- Before beginning a lesson, conduct a very brief review of previously achieved, related learning.
- Facilitates storage of information in long-term memory.
- Helps connect old learning to new.
- Indicates when reteaching is necessary.

Examples	Nonexamples
• Sample the understanding of a "steering group." • Lead an overt review/practice.	• Ask students, "Do you remember last week when we learned how to use a ruler?" and move on. • State, "On Friday we learned the sound the letter *b* makes" and move on.

FIGURE 6.2   Review Previously Learned Skills.

students about key points from the earlier lesson and ask students to complete a few quick examples before beginning the new one. However, if a new skill or concept is being introduced that depends on skills learned much earlier, more elaborate review and assessment of prerequisite skills may be needed. Consider the following examples of daily review strategies:

- If today's lesson is a direct continuation of yesterday's and you are reasonably sure that students understood yesterday's lesson, begin with a quick reminder about the earlier lesson by asking a few quick questions:

  "Yesterday we learned how to add the suffix -ed to a word ending in y. Think for a moment about how this is done. Then raise your hand and be prepared to explain."

- If a new skill is being introduced that depends on skills learned much earlier, a more elaborate discussion and explicit review of the task-relevant information is necessary before the day's lesson:

  "Let's review subtraction when we have enough ones." Put on the chalkboard and *have all students solve:*

$$47 \quad 56 \quad 89$$
$$\underline{-3} \quad \underline{-4} \quad \underline{-8}$$

  Give answers, discuss all items missed by many students.

- Sample the understanding of a steering group: a few low-, average-, and high-performing students who are probably good indicators of the range of knowledge possessed by the entire class. When high performers miss a large proportion of answers at the start of the class, this is a warning that extensive reteaching for the entire class is necessary. When high performers answer correctly but average performers do not, some reteaching should be done. Finally, if most of the high and average performers answer correctly but most of the low performers do not, then individualized reteaching is needed for low performers. This ensures that large amounts of large-group instructional time are not devoted to review and reteaching that may benefit only a small number of students.

PRETEACH KEY VOCABULARY

As teachers, we want students to understand a wide range of words. A key to successful learning is quick, fluent access to word meanings. Brief preteaching of new vocabulary can set students up for success by fostering fluency and prevent them from faltering over unknown words or terms during reading or instruction (Marzano & Pickering, 2005) (see Figure 6.3).

Vocabulary acquisition is fostered not by one approach but by a combination of approaches. Research suggests that e.i. is more effective than incidental learning for the acquisition of new vocabulary (Reutzel & Hollingsworth, 1988), but the combination of both incidental learning from context and e.i. is likely to be more effective than either strategy alone (Nagy & Herman, 1987). This means that teachers need to encourage students to continue to expand their concepts of words on their own as well as providing instruction that helps students process new words more deeply.

New words can be introduced prior to the first-time reading of trade books or basal stories. Words that should be pretaught are those that are relatively high in frequency, that are

---

☐ 2 to 10 minutes

Essential Characteristics

- Prevents students from puzzling over difficult words during instruction.
- Text: preview words that appear most frequently or that students will not be able to figure out given their current skill level.
- Lesson: preview vocabulary central to the content being taught.
- Two or three words in the primary grades; 3–5 words in the intermediate grades.

Examples	Nonexamples
• Preview in Context: • Select unfamiliar words. • Present in context. • Discuss in context. • Expand meanings. • Directly instruct students to decode new words and recite their meanings.	• Read unfamiliar words and definitions from a list of 20 words. • Preview the word *boy* instead of the word *gingerbread*. • Post unfamiliar words but do not refer to them. • Preview *all* the new words in a text or lesson. • Look up words in the dictionary and write the definitions.

FIGURE 6.3 Preteach Key Vocabulary.

hard to identify using context and/or pictures, and that the student does not yet have the skills to decode. It is not necessary to preteach *all* the words in the story that students cannot yet recognize. Rather, select those that occur most frequently and that students will probably not be able to figure out given their current skills and strategies.

Readence, Bean, and Baldwin (2004) suggested the use of the preteaching strategy "Preview in Context." This strategy asks students to look at words in context, giving them a better understanding of the specific definition of the word that will be used. Discussing key words ahead of time also gives students the opportunity to develop background knowledge for the topic to be read or discussed. Preview in Context has several key characteristics:

- Select words from the text or lesson that you think will be unfamiliar to students. Make sure to choose words that are key to the understanding of the text and don't make the list too long. It is better to have an effective lesson with a few words (two or three in the primary grades and four or five in the intermediate grades) than to have a lesson of 10 words that students forget.
- As with reviewing task-relevant material, the rate of presentation for previewing key vocabulary should be quick and effective, leaving the majority of instructional time for achievement of the current objective.
- Show students the words in context (e.g., in the text sentence in which it appears).
- Help students learn the word meaning by briefly discussing it in its context. You may want to ask questions to help lead the students to the definition.
- Expand word meanings. After students learn the initial meaning of the word, provide additional contexts for the same word. That way, when students encounter the word in a different context, they will make predictions on the basis of what they know about the word's meaning.
- Keep in mind that preteaching important vocabulary is one brief component of an e.i. lesson. It is not always possible or sensible to preview in context (e.g., when introducing new math terms). However, it is important to give students the opportunity to interact with new words by providing some e.i. and a great deal of practice reading new words.
- Have fun with new words. Students learn by the example you set. If you enjoy learning the meanings of new words or enjoy the sounds of words, your students will also become excited about words.

Nonexamples of Preteaching Key Vocabulary

- Read unfamiliar words and definitions from a list of 20 words.
- Preview the word *boy* instead of the word *gingerbread*.
- Post unfamiliar words but do not refer to them.
- Preview *all* the new words in a text or lesson.
- Look up words in the dictionary and write the definitions.

Summary

This chapter discussed three elements that can be used to prepare the knowledge base for instruction: activate prior knowledge, review previously learned skills, and preteach key vocabulary. Remember that you will not include all three of these elements in a single e.i. lesson but rather choose the most appropriate option depending on the learning objective. Now let's put it all together. Here is an example of a review from a kindergarten math lesson:

> "During yesterday's math lesson we learned that inches are the major component of a standard ruler. Many everyday items are measured in inches using rulers. Look at your rulers. Remember, each long line on the ruler equals 1 inch. How many inches are found on a standard ruler? Please close your eyes and think about the answer to this question. When I come to you and tap your shoulder, please whisper your answer in my ear." Give the students a few seconds to construct their answers. "I will begin on the left side of our semicircle. Please be prepared to give me your answer when I get to you." This quick form of assessment will determine whether you need to reteach yesterday's math lesson on the ruler. "Good! Most of you told me that a ruler contains 12 inches. This information will help us today when we will learn how to properly measure different objects to the nearest inch."

Review

1. How does prior knowledge relate to learning new material?
2. What are some strategies for actively involving all students in the activation of prior knowledge?
3. How can accessing prior knowledge help students who tend to be easily frustrated?
4. Why is reviewing especially important for less capable learners?
5. What should you do if certain students cannot handle the same material and move ahead at the same pace as the rest of the class? What might you do differently with these students? How might you explain it to them in ways that would support rather than undermine their motivation to learn?
6. What does research suggest about the benefits of incidental versus direct teaching of new vocabulary?
7. What kinds of words are especially useful to preteach?

Apply

1. You are introducing the study of pollution and the environment to your class. It is important to see what your students already know about this topic. Write a detailed plan for how you would access/activate your students' background knowledge.
2. Using a copy of a familiar text, write a detailed plan for how you would use the Preview in Context strategy to preteach two or three key vocabulary words before beginning a small-group reading lesson.
3. Following these directions are two hypothetical teaching situations. Choose one and script a review of prerequisite skills that you feel would work effectively in that situation.

   a. Situation A: Your class has been working on a math unit in measurement. During the first lesson, the students learned to measure the length of classroom objects using nonstandard units (e.g., pencils, paper clips, and paper strips). The second lesson of the unit will be measuring length using a ruler.
   b. Situation B: You class has been studying the letters *b*, *s*, and *m*. You wish to introduce the letter *l* today.

CHAPTER 7

Instruction

At this point, you have introduced the lesson to your students and prepared the knowledge base for new learning. Everything that has been done prior to this moment has laid important cognitive groundwork for the presentation of new skills, strategies, or content. The explicit instruction (e.i.) elements presented in this chapter represent the culmination of an e.i. lesson. This chapter is called "Instruction" because it is the part of the lesson where the majority of new information is explicitly presented. Instruction includes three teaching skills: cognitive modeling, guided and independent practice, and closure.

The length of this portion of the lesson will vary depending on the developmental level of your students. For example, in elementary school, teachers may model and engage students in guided practice, independent practice, and closure all within a 10- to 15-minute time frame (see Figure 7.1). In secondary school, however, it may take several days to complete all the parts of the lesson.

COGNITIVE MODELING

Research on the strategic and metacognitive aspects of learning underscores the need for modeling not only the physical, observable aspects of a task, but also the invisible mental processes that underlie it (Duffy et al., 1988; Pressley, Forrest-Pressley, Elliott-Faust, & Miller, 1985). For example, people's thought process while reading is not something that can be readily observed; just observing a reader scanning a page and then turning it gives no indication of the activity going on in the reader's mind. To reveal the thinking process, teachers verbalize their own thoughts or "think aloud"—making their thought process visible to learners. Students are required to watch observable behaviors as the instructor performs a task and to

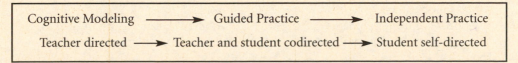

FIGURE 7.1 Relinquishing Teacher Control During Instruction.

listen to the instructor's self-talk. Through the detailed process of making thinking public, the teacher models both observable behaviors and the unobservable thinking processes associated with those behaviors. In this way, students are made aware of different strategies they can use. In addition, the possibility that students will misinterpret the teacher's instruction is minimized.

Being able to model unobservable thinking processes is a key component for teaching such cognitive skills as reading strategies, math problem solving, editing and revising written work, and even solving social dilemmas. This method helps students see that the answer to a problem is a logical conclusion following a sequence of reasoning rather than something the teacher "just knew" that the student must commit to memory (which, for some students, may be next to impossible). Cognitive modeling may be used in many different ways. The teacher might model self-monitoring and self-reinforcement statements (e.g., "Oh, I made a mistake. How can I go back and correct it?"), accessing prior knowledge and help (e.g., "Let me think back to what I already know about solving problems like this."), summarizing important information and planning ("Now I've finished steps 1, 2, and 3. Let me read step 4 and think about where to start."), and domain-specific modeling associated with a particular task, such as reading or math computation. ("When I come to a word I don't know, I think about the strategies I've already learned. For example, I can look at the picture for a clue.") In the course of modeling, the teacher may use one of these approaches or combine them (see Figure 7.2).

Whichever form of cognitive modeling you choose, be sure that you model the learning objective that is the focus of your lesson. This may seem like an unnecessary caveat; however,

☐ 10 minutes to ?

Essential Characteristics

- The detailed process of making thinking public or "thinking aloud."
- Students see that the answer to a problem is a logical conclusion following a sequence of reasoning.
- Two kinds of think alouds:
  a. Self-questioning—perform task while asking self-guiding questions.
  b. Self-directive—perform task while giving self-directive prompts.
- * Organize thinking before, during, and after performing a task.

Examples	Nonexamples
• Physically performing the task while verbally guided oneself. • Describe each individual step and its importance. • Make predictions. • Verbalize confusing points. • Demonstrate "fix-up" strategies.	• Model but do not use think-aloud. • Present general background information only. • Model only in response to student errors. • * Model a skill/strategy unrelated to the current instructional objective.

FIGURE 7.2 Cognitive Modeling.

teachers sometimes become confused about exactly what it is they are supposed to be modeling. For example, when teaching a lesson on syllabication, a beginning teacher models how to clap out the number of syllables in a word but not how syllabication can be used as a decoding strategy. This is a common mistake that typically emerges from teachers' lack of familiarity with making their thinking public. We are used to teaching students how to follow procedures; we may be less familiar with the process of teaching students how to think.

Although some concepts or procedures can be demonstrated with little or no verbalization, modeling is most effective when accompanied by verbal explanations. This procedure may seem obvious, but many teachers do not teach this way. Some teachers are uncomfortable modeling a strategy or procedure one time through without student input (again, they worry about uninterrupted segments of teacher talk). Instead, they partially model and then stop to ask, "What should I do next? Who knows the answer?" This type of modeling constitutes a well-intentioned effort to involve students in your teaching. What this type of modeling fails to acknowledge is that many students may not already know the answer. There will be certain students who need to see and hear one smooth, uninterrupted model in order to learn well. Such students will benefit from a complete and thorough cognitive model by the teacher before student input into the process is solicited. Since many students can benefit from repeated modeling, you might consider modeling one time through first using self-directive statements (e.g., "The first thing I should do is . . ."), followed by a second example using self-questioning with student input (e.g., "What should I do next?"). In this way, the teacher can promote the thinking and problem-solving processes that help all students learn how to find the answer.

Occasionally, I encounter teachers who feel uncomfortable with modeling because it closely resembles traditional teaching methods that "impart" knowledge. We are taught that democratic, student-centered teaching involves guiding students to reach their own conclusions. If we model, aren't we implicitly telling students that our way is the only correct way of doing something? In inclusive classrooms, teaching is student centered to the extent that it is effective for helping each individual student progress toward independent, self-directed learning. Once again, it is important to remember for whom e.i. is intended: students who need to acquire or accelerate progress toward mastery of skills, strategies, or content. If students can acquire and master one way of doing something, eventually they may be able to discover alternative strategies. At their current level of mastery, however, it is unlikely that they will be able to do so without e.i.

An additional consideration during cognitive modeling is the importance of examples and nonexamples. Customarily, teachers will give examples of a concept they are trying to teach, but they don't always think to provide students with nonexamples. Providing nonexamples requires anticipatory teaching because you must think ahead to how students might confuse the concept and provide useful nonexamples that will help them to filter out any potential misunderstandings. For example, let's say you were going to teach the concept of an "island." You might list the critical attributes of an island on a chart so that students can refer to it as a prompt: (a) landmass (not a continent), (b) water, and (c) land surrounded by water. In addition to the list, you might show a simple drawing in which only the critical attributes are labeled and point out each critical attribute. This could be followed by pictures of best examples, such as Hawaii, Greenland, or Cuba. As each picture is presented, you would think aloud about why each is a good example of an island, pointing out the critical attributes again. Next, you might show students both examples and nonexamples and ask questions that elicit judgments about whether each new picture is an example or a nonexample of an island. Students would have to justify their judgments by telling why or why not.

Eventually, they could even come up with their own examples and nonexamples. The number of examples and nonexamples used will depend on the extent of students' demonstrated understanding.

The cognitive modeling portion of a lesson most often involves the following characteristics:

- Both physically performing the skill or skills required for the task and verbally guiding oneself or thinking aloud while carrying out the task. The task could be overt (e.g., how to measure an object with a ruler) or covert (e.g., how to make an inference when reading a narrative text). In either case, the teacher's job is to make the internal cognitive processes explicit.
- Rate of presentation is deliberate. Any procedures or actions are performed slowly and with exaggerated motions.
- Cognitive modeling may take two forms: self-questioning (e.g., "What do I need to do next?") or self-directive statements (e.g., "The first thing I should do is . . .") (Meichenbaum & Beimiller, 1998).
- Think-alouds describe each individual step in a process and highlight the importance of each step using verbal cues (e.g., First, I. . . . Second, I. . . . Next, I should. . . . At the end, I go back and . . .).
- Modeling is structured according to what you think before, during, and after carrying out a particular task; inappropriate structuring (e.g., explaining the task as one big step) is apt to overwhelm students. Use task-directive terms that mirror this structure: first, next, then, at the end, and so on.

Examples of Teacher Statements During Cognitive Modeling

- Model what you are thinking before, during, and after carrying out the task:
    a. "My first step is. . . . Next I . . ."
    b. "Watch while I do this, and I'll tell you what I'm thinking as I work . . ."
    c. "What we might do now is go back and self-check . . ."
- Select a story to read aloud that contains unknown words. As the teacher reads the story aloud, students follow along silently, listening to how the teacher thinks through each trouble spot.
- Make predictions:
    a. "From the title, I predict that this story will tell how Arthur got the chicken pox."
    b. "In this next part, I think we'll find out why Charlie found the golden ticket."
    c. "I think this is a description of the countryside."
- Develop images. Describe the picture you're forming in your head from the information:
    a. "I have a picture of this scene in my mind. The animals are all crowded into the mitten. It's getting very tight and hot with all those furry animals in there!"
- Incorporate multiple examples and nonexamples.
- Verbalize confusing points:
    a. "This just doesn't make sense."
    b. "This is different from what I expected."
    c. "I'm getting confused. Let me see if I understand what I'm supposed to do . . ."
- Demonstrate "fix-up" strategies:
    a. "I'd better go back and do it again."
    b. "This word is new to me. I'd better check the sentence to figure it out."

   c. "That didn't work, so now I'll try . . ."
   d. "What can I do if I need help?"

Nonexamples of Cognitive Modeling

- Model but do not think aloud
- Present general background information only
- Model only in response to student errors
- Model a skill/strategy unrelated to the current instructional objective
- Model directions rather than learning (e.g., explain how to make a clock out of a paper plate rather than how to tell time to the hour)

GUIDED AND INDEPENDENT PRACTICE

We have all heard the phrase "practice makes perfect." In cognitive terms, practice serves as the rehearsal for transferring information from working memory into long-term memory. The instruction portion of an e.i. lesson can be conceptualized on a continuum that starts out as highly teacher directed during cognitive modeling, becomes teacher and student codirected during guided practice, and becomes student directed during independent practice (see Figure 7.3). From the beginning of the lesson, the teacher's ultimate goal is for students to engage in accurate, self-directed independent practice. If initial errors become engrained in working memory, they can be difficult to modify. The beginning stages of learning, therefore, are critical for determining successful future performance. As a result, students' initial attempts at practice should be carefully monitored and guided so that they are accurate and successful (Hunter, 1994). As students become more competent, the teacher gradually relinquishes control in favor of student self-direction during independent practice.

☐ 5 minutes to ?

Essential Characteristics

- Immediately follows presentation and modeling of initial concept.
- Promotes and solidifies learning achieved during earlier part of the lesson.
- Directly linked to learning objective.
- Active participation.
- Promotes student self-direction.

Examples	Nonexamples
• Practice with peers. • Group problem solving or application. • Teacher-directed individual guided practice.	• Worksheet activity at the beginning of a lesson. • *Practicing errors when working independently.

FIGURE 7.3 Guided and Independent Practice.

Practice activities are especially helpful for students with special needs because they provide extended engaged time and help promote deeper understanding of new learning. Once students are engaged in guided practice, the teacher should circulate among the class or group to make sure that instruction has "taken" before setting students free to practice independently (with limited or no help available). With teacher guidance, students need to perform all (or enough) of the task so that clarification or remediation can occur promptly if needed. In this way, the teacher can be sure that students will perform the task correctly during independent practice rather than practicing errors when working by themselves.

Guided practice is most appropriate immediately following cognitive modeling of the skill, strategy, or concept. There are several ways that teacher-organized guided practice can be accomplished, such as practice with peer partners, group problem solving or application, or teacher-monitored individual guided practice (see Table 7.1). Guided practice should be conducted in as nonevaluative an atmosphere as possible. Students should be free to risk giving incorrect responses out of which you can begin to coconstruct an accurate understanding. Any response, however inexpert or clumsy, can be the basis for learning if it is supported by appropriate corrective feedback.

In order to be successful, practice activities must be directly aligned with the learning objective. Guided practice that does not allow students to practice the learning objective or that is indirectly related to the objective will not improve student learning. For example, Darcy, a beginning first-grade teacher, taught a science lesson in which students learned the stages in the life cycle of a butterfly. She sent students back to their seats with the direction that they should rewrite and illustrate the stages in order. At each table, she provided a prompt for the students; however, the prompt listed the stages out of order, and the practice task was for students to write them in order. Darcy had omitted this from her explanation, thinking that requiring students to "figure it out" would show who really understood her lesson. On finally "figuring it out," one student remarked, "I think it was a trick!" It is only a trick if you don't explain it clearly. Students should practice precisely what you teach and model.

In addition to alignment with the learning objective, a successful guided practice activity includes several other characteristics:

- Guided practice activities must be used to promote learning that occurred during the earlier part of the lesson; in other words, avoid throwing students a curveball by introducing new information or skills during guided practice.

TABLE 7.1 Examples of Guided Practice Activities

Objective	Guided Practice Activity
Writing consonant–vowel–consonant words in cursive for handwriting practice	Dictation by teacher, work checked after every sentence
Solving math word problems with the word "more"	Students solve problems one at a time while the teacher monitors their execution of each step
Measuring with yardsticks to make a scale model of the classroom	Teacher-led group problem solving
Figuring out unknown words by reading to the end of the sentence and going back	Practice with peers

- Students with disabilities or complex learning needs are less likely to learn new information from worksheet-type activities. Although worksheets are a convenience at times, guided practice activities should be varied to enhance and extend meaningful participation by all students.
- Rate of presentation for guided practice should be deliberate while promoting the active participation of all students. Keep the pace and enthusiasm as high as possible during guided practice (e.g., "Everyone who thinks they know the answer, put your thumbs up!").

Nonexamples of Guided Practice Activities

- Worksheet activity at the beginning of a lesson
- Omitting guided practice so that students practice errors when working independently
- Guided practice for how to correctly put glue on paper (or some other activity that is not central to the learning objective)

Once the teacher and students have completed enough guided practice to facilitate independent performance, it is time to check students' understanding (see Chapter 4) and then reinforce individual proficiency with the new skill, strategy, or concept. At times, your check of student understanding may indicate that many students are still unclear. Always be prepared to provide additional guided practice when needed.

In contrast to guided practice, which is done with scaffolded teacher support, independent practice is self-directed: students work independently with little or no teacher interaction. For younger students, independent practice may be group or individual work done in class. In middle and secondary school, independent practice often takes the form of homework.

In inclusive classrooms in particular, independent practice still requires some teacher monitoring. You do not want the outcome of your carefully crafted e.i. lesson to be that some students practice errors that then become entrenched and difficult to reverse. This makes your instructional job even harder. During independent practice, teacher monitoring may consist of a quick sweep around the classroom as students begin to work independently. The teacher can immediately identify those who are having difficulty getting started and provide a small group with additional guided practice if needed.

If independent practice takes the form of written homework, obviously the teacher cannot provide additional monitoring. In that case, however, you might consider providing a procedural prompt along with one or two completed examples at the top of the homework page. This not only helps parents who may be assisting their children at home but also serves as a review for students who may have difficulty remembering back to what happened in class. Teachers are sometimes reluctant to provide such prompts, reasoning that students should have class notes to which they can refer for help. However, this conclusion includes several assumptions: (a) that students took adequate and legible notes to be able to understand when looking back, (b) that students brought their notebooks home with them, and (c) that even if the students did bring their notebooks home, they make the link between looking at their notes and completing the homework successfully. If independent practice routinely consists of homework and some students consistently fail to complete it out of frustration or confusion, you might consider creative ways to promote successful, self-directed independent performance.

Independent practice is not always written. Particularly in inclusive classrooms, teachers should work to provide students with multiple means for expressing their learning.

Independent practice should be provided in enough different contexts that skills, strategies, and concepts can be generalized to subsequent contexts—not only those in which they were originally learned. Failure to help students generalize skills and strategies is part of the reason why so many students are unable to apply their learning meaningfully in new settings.

At different times, independent practice activities may be skill based (e.g., worksheet, flash cards, game, or drill) or application based (e.g., journal entry, essay, diorama, PowerPoint presentation, dramatization, or oral presentation). Skill-based practice activities promote mastery—quick, accurate, fluent performance of skills or procedures. Application-based practice activities promote generalization to meaningful, real-life settings. Rather than consistently relying on one form of practice (e.g., worksheets), teachers can combine skill-based and application-based activities to provide students with a variety of engaging and constructive independent practice opportunities.

CLOSURE

Closure is an action, a statement, or an activity that is designed to bring an e.i. lesson to an appropriate and satisfying conclusion. Closure has several purposes. It is used to help organize student learning and facilitate storage and retrieval of the skill, strategy, or concept that has just been taught. It helps students become reflective learners by requiring them to actively consider what happened in class. Closure is also the last opportunity the teacher has during the lesson to gauge student understanding and clear up any lingering misunderstandings. Teachers will sometimes sacrifice closure in deference to classroom time constraints, particularly in secondary settings where class periods are fairly short and there is a lot of content to cover. However, the end or closure of a lesson is just as important as the beginning. Lessons that omit or include weak closure deny students the opportunity to think about and discuss what they have learned and deny the teacher important formative assessment data about the extent of student understanding (see Figure 7.4).

Weak forms of closure include asking students if there are any questions and moving on (e.g., "Are there any questions? Then let's move on to Science.") or a brief lecture, summary, or "wrap-up" statement made by the teacher (e.g., "Today you learned how to use a protractor. Here are the three take-home points . . ."). These types of statements provide closure for the teacher; however, passive students may or may not be listening and are left without a meaningful conclusion to the lesson. Like other components of e.i., effective closure is active and allows students to demonstrate their grasp of the learning objective. It should leave students with a meaningful sense of what has just been learned. In other words, you want students to go away from your lesson with whatever skill, strategy, or concept they just learned in the forefront of their minds. As a result, they will be much more likely to be able to recall the information the next time they need to use it.

For older students, closure consists of more synthesis than review. In other words, older students might be required to apply or elaborate their learning by summarizing or considering how the learning fits with what they already know about the topic. One strategy for this type of synthesis is the "three whats":

1. What did we learn today? (review and summarize)
2. So what? (how is it important, relevant, or useful?)
3. Now what? (how does it relate to our unit outcomes?)

☐ 1 to 5 minutes

Essential Characteristics

- Check that students have information they need to work on their own and achieve the instructional objective.
- Facilitates storage and retrieval of new information.
- * Provides quick teacher data: Is more practice needed? Do I need to reteach? Can I go on?

Examples	Nonexamples
• Signaled response. • Sampling. • Individual private response (e.g., think–pair–share). • Individual verbal response (e.g., classroom whip-around). • Quick pencil-and-paper activity (e.g., "door pass," problem of the day, response card, learning journal, or Lesson Closure Summary Sheet; see Table 7.2). • * Statement from students of what they learned in the lesson (e.g., the three whats or "3–2–1": three things they found interesting, two things they learned, and one thing they still have a question about).	• "Let's move on to social studies." • "Today you learned to read a thermometer." • "Are there any questions?" • "Please put your math books away." • * Passive review in which students look and listen as teacher rereads key points.

FIGURE 7.4   Closure.

Examples of Effective Closure Activities

- Signaled response
- Sampling
- Individual private response (e.g., think–pair–share)
- Individual verbal response (e.g., classroom whip-around)
- Quick pencil-and-paper and activity (e.g., "door pass," problem of the day, response card, learning journal, or Lesson Closure Summary Sheet; see Table 7.2)
- Statement from students of what they learned in the lesson (e.g., the three whats or "3–2–1": three things they found interesting, two things they learned, and one thing they still have a question about)

TABLE 7.2   Lesson Closure Summary Sheet

Today's lesson was about _____. One

important point was _____. This

is important because _____.

_____In sum, today I learned _____.

Nonexamples of Closure

- "Let's move on to social studies."
- "Today you learned how to turn a liquid into a gas."
- "Are there any questions?"
- "Please put your math books away."
- Passive review in which students listen as the teacher rereads key points.

Summary

This chapter discussed the three elements of instruction, the critical final portion of an e.i. lesson: cognitive modeling, guided and independent practice, and closure. Remember that you should check students' understanding throughout e.i. but especially before releasing students to engage in independent practice. Let's look at an example of instruction from an elementary math lesson in which students are taught three different ways to state time to the half hour:

Cognitive model: [Holding the large Judy clock in front of the class showing the time 1:30.] "Whenever we use the term 'half hour,' the minute hand will always be pointing to the 6 on the clock. I have to think to myself that when counting by 5s, I know that the 6 stands for 30." I'll model this by taking the minute hand, putting it on the 12, and counting by 5s until I reach the 6. "Notice on my clock that the hour hand is pointing in between the 1 and 2 and that the minute hand is pointing to the 6. This means 1:30. Now there are three different ways to say times to the half hour. Look at this

chart. One way to say 1:30 would be half past 1. Another way of saying 1:30 is 30 minutes after 1. The final and tricky way to say 1:30 is 30 minutes before 2 because in thirty minutes it will be 2:00. These are the three ways of showing a time to the half hour. I am going to leave this chart on the board to help you during guided practice and independent practice."

Guided practice: "I am going to say a time. With your partner, you are going to show me that time on each of your clocks. Remember to discuss your answer with your partner before setting your clocks." Model how to do this with a student in the class. "Thumbs up if you are ready to begin. Excellent! I want you to show me 30 minutes past 7." Students will discuss time with partner and set time on miniclocks. "Five seconds. Okay, raise your clocks." Continue this method with various ways of saying a half hour.

Check student understanding: Check student understanding by walking around while the partners are discussing the correct way to show the time on the clock. While doing this, I will be able to help the students if they are confused. In addition, by raising the clocks after each time, I am using active participation to determine whether all students have grasped the concept.

Independent practice: "Boys and girls, you did a great job telling time to the half hour. Now you are going to practice this skill on your own. I am going to pass out these cards, and once everyone has their deck, we will go over the directions together." Pass out one deck of cards to each student. "You have a deck of cards. Some of the cards in the deck show clock faces to the half hour [show example]. Other cards show times in standard notation or in words [show examples]. You are going to match the clock faces to the cards that show the time either in standard notation or in words. Watch me." Model how to do one example. "When you're done, you should have 10 matched pairs. Once you have

matched all of your pairs and checked your work, raise your hand, and I will come to your desk to check your work." As students begin working, the teacher makes a sweep around the classroom to identify those who may need additional support.

Closure: "Everyone, please turn over your worksheets. I am going to give you an index card. Your card may have a time written on it, like 10:30. Or it may have one of the ways we can say time to the half hour on it, like '30 minutes before 11.' When I say go, you are going to look at your card and then try to find the other people in the group whose cards goes with yours. In the end, there will be four people in your group with four different cards: one with a digital time and three others with the three ways of saying the time. When you've found your group members, sit together on the carpet. You will have 5 minutes. Go!" Students find their group members and share with the whole group.

Review

1. Why does cognitive modeling have a powerful influence on student learning?
2. Describe in your own words the steps that are included in an effective cognitive model or think-aloud.
3. In cognitive terms, why are guided and independent practice important for student learning?
4. What are some ways that guided practice can be accomplished?
5. What are the characteristics of an appropriate closure activity?

Apply

1. You are preparing to read a familiar text to your students, and you wish to model or "think aloud" the reading strategy of prediction. Write a detailed plan for how you would use a think-aloud to model this strategy.
2. You are teaching a math lesson on recognizing sets. You have explained that a set is a group of like objects and have shown some examples (e.g., pencils, chalk, and other classroom items) and nonexamples. Now you are ready for guided practice. Each student has a pile of multicolored

lifesaver candies and a few lengths of yarn. Write a detailed plan for how you would engage your students in guided practice.
3. You are at the conclusion of a secondary history lesson on factors that led to the Great Depression. Students have just completed independent practice in which they completed a time line listing each factor and when it occurred. There are 5 minutes left for you to conduct a closure activity. Write a detailed plan for how you would engage your students in active closure for this lesson.

PART THREE

Applications of Explicit Instruction

CHAPTER 8

Explicit Instruction in Literacy

Now that the explicit instruction (e.i.) framework has been presented, the next two chapters discuss how e.i. can be situated within classroom instruction as a whole. As stated previously, the purpose of this book is not to say that a steady diet of e.i. is the ideal instructional prescription for all students. Rather, this book is designed to help you become skilled at conducting e.i. lessons and to help you apply e.i. strategically in order to meet individual students' needs. In other words, e.i. is one critical approach to have in your teaching repertoire. Effective teachers know when to apply it, how much, and in combination with what other instructional approaches in order to accelerate student progress. This chapter discusses how e.i. can be used in the language arts.

THE IMPORTANCE OF e.i. IN READING

Teacher-led instruction has been nowhere more hotly debated than in the field of reading. Reading instruction has been significantly influenced by two seemingly incompatible bodies of research, one advocating a strong focus on meaning and the other advocating for e.i. in phonemic awareness and other foundational skills. Meaning-based approaches such as whole-language and literature-based teaching are grounded in a belief system that centers student's interests. These approaches attempt to mobilize student interest in reading through developmentally appropriate, literature-rich environments (Goodman, 2005). According to this view, students learn to read by recognizing contextual cues, such as story themes or pictures, and structural cues, such as word types (e.g., verbs or nouns). Through their own unique interactions with the literacy immersion process, students are believed to construct meaning from texts naturally, without planned or intrusive instruction by teachers. Explicit attention is not paid to the teaching of discrete reading skills and strategies. Literacy learning is assessed informally through teacher observation rather than standard measures. In summary, this type of approach espouses a certain broad set of beliefs about education in general—in particular, value and respect for young children as free, self-directed learners and for their teachers as autonomous decision makers.

In contrast, e.i. approaches to reading emphasize (a) that the alphabetic principle cannot be obtained by most students, particularly those who are at risk or have disabilities, simply through immersion or exposure to literature; (b) that skills in decoding provide the critical foundation for being able to derive meaning from text and engage in imaginative, independent reading; (c) that literacy teaching is best done by skilled experts; and (d) that instructional decisions are based on student data rather than teacher opinion or observation (National Institute of Child Health and Human Development, 2000). Despite ongoing controversy, the research base for e.i. in reading is unusually solid. Research and evaluation studies carried out using a variety of methods in diverse settings over a period of more than 25 years has shown that e.i. approaches have a strong, positive effect on student achievement in reading as measured by tests of decoding, comprehension, and attitudes toward reading (Carnine, Silbert, & Kameenui, 1997; Foorman, Francis, Fletcher, Schatschneider, & Mehta, 1998; Foorman & Torgesen, 2001; NRP, 2000).

The dichotomy between holistic and explicit approaches is perpetuated when general educators are trained in holistic teaching methods and special educators are trained in e.i. methods. Neither method is wrong for the purpose for which it was developed; on the other hand, neither method is the right one for all students. For example, students should be exposed to vibrant children's literature, engaged in meaningful literacy activities, and interact in stimulating, enriching environments. These aspects of holistic approaches to reading are part of what makes literacy learning meaningful and fun. It is important to note, however, that one of the most consistent findings to emerge from the past decade of reading research is the relationship among phonemic awareness, reading acquisition, and later reading success (Adams, 1990). Students who lack phonemic awareness skills as a precursor to learning to read are at risk for developing reading disabilities. These students need e.i. in literacy if they are to become skilled readers and spellers.

Techniques that target phonemic awareness most frequently involve e.i. in segmenting words into component sounds, identifying sounds in various positions in words (i.e., initial, medial, and final), identifying words that begin or end with the same sound, and manipulating sounds in a word, such as saying a word without its beginning or ending sound (e.g., "Say *mat* without the /t/."). A fundamental tenet of holistic approaches to reading instruction is that word analysis skills should only arise incidentally in the context of reading connected text (i.e., the "teachable moment"). As a result, some general educators resist incorporating explicit phonemic awareness and phonics instruction into their reading programs. Although special educators have the requisite background in e.i., the students most in need of this instruction— young beginning readers who lack phonemic awareness skills—are usually found in general education classrooms. It is critical, therefore, that general educators engage in ongoing assessment to identify students who need e.i. as part of their instructional program in reading.

More recently, educators have begun to realize that perhaps no single approach to reading instruction is superior to the others or best for all students. In fact, characteristics of the teacher and the individual learners may be more salient considerations than the method employed (Bond & Dykstra, 1997). Comprehensive approaches to the teaching of reading offer several benefits to teachers in inclusive classrooms, including (a) an alternative to the extremes of pure whole-language or skill-based approaches, (b) helping teachers think about an effective combination of approaches rather than a single "right" approach for their students, and (c) accommodating a range of different learning needs within the general education classroom (Pressley, 1998; Weaver, 1998).

Typically, a comprehensive approach means components of both literature-based and skill-based methods are combined in order to meet students' individual needs. Researchers assert—and most practitioners agree—that beginning readers need to learn both phonemic awareness (knowledge of the sound system of language) and reading strategies (how to decode and comprehend text). The essence of an effective, balanced reading program is the relationship between systematic, explicit skills instruction and literature, language, and comprehension. While skills alone are insufficient to develop competent readers, no reader can become proficient without these foundational skills (Honig, 1996). Therefore, teachers who emphasize whole-language approaches must be careful to balance their reading program with explicit phonics instruction for those who need it; teachers who favor code-based approaches must provide a complement of enriching, meaningful experiences with literature and writing. The challenge becomes where to situate e.i. in a comprehensive reading instruction program— whether to separate it and teach reading skills and strategies in isolation or to provide e.i. within an integrated language arts program. Lapp and Flood (1998) support the notion that phonics should be taught both explicitly and contextually, reinforcing what students already know and providing instruction in new skills and content.

In the literature at present, the meaning of comprehensive reading instruction is best illustrated through examples of classroom practice rather than research-based reports. One classroom-based example of this kind of approach was described by Cunningham and Hall (2000). They conceptualized a balanced literacy framework as consisting of four blocks (see Figure 8.1). Each of the four blocks is based on one of the major historical approaches to reading instruction. As such, instructional time devoted to language arts is divided equally among the four blocks (30 to 40 minutes each): (a) guided reading, (b) self-selected reading, (c) writers workshop, and (d) working with words. Within this type of framework, contextual teaching of phonics might occur throughout all four blocks, with e.i. occurring regularly during working with words.

An effective comprehensive reading program involves more than structuring instructional time appropriately. Teachers must also be familiar with the instructional objectives for the grade they are teaching as well those of a grade below and a grade above (Strickland, 1998). The

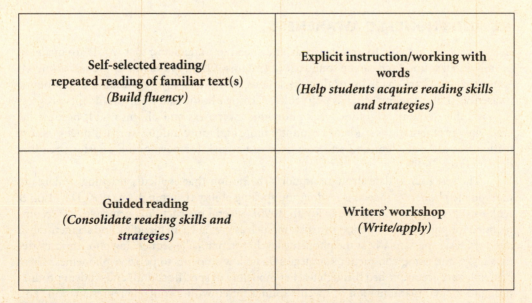

Self-selected reading/ repeated reading of familiar text(s) (*Build fluency*)	Explicit instruction/working with words (*Help students acquire reading skills and strategies*)
Guided reading (*Consolidate reading skills and strategies*)	Writers' workshop (*Write/apply*)

FIGURE 8.1   Suggested Language Arts Format (Based on the Four Blocks).

adoption of statewide standards for language arts has attempted to establish coherent expectations and accountability for student achievement. Standards vary widely, however, in terms of their quality, rigor, and specificity regarding reading requirements, literacy skills, and pedagogical approaches. Therefore, teachers must be prepared to align their classroom practice with clearly defined research-based standards for reading instruction, whether or not these are well explicated in their state's language arts standards or their school district's curricula.

One source of research-based information on reading instruction is data from the NRP (2000). This panel was formed by Congress largely in response to the "reading wars" and out of concern that many students in the nation's schools were not learning to read. In 2000, the NRP released its report of the most effective methods for teaching students to read. The panel was charged with investigating what works in classroom practice; as a result, they examined studies that attempted to try out programs, methods, or techniques in classroom conditions to determine their impact on learning. Charged with discovering "what works," the panel examined data that, in their judgment, might best answer that question. The panel's report has been met with controversy, specifically regarding what constitutes "research-based" instruction in reading.

Despite the controversy, the NRP report constitutes one of the most comprehensive and rigorous analyses of data we have to date regarding what works in helping students learn to read. The NRP concluded that effective reading instruction consists of five key components: phonemic awareness, phonics, vocabulary development, fluency, and comprehension. The following sections consist of brief descriptions of e.i. as it relates to each of these components. Although these are foundational skills that would most often be taught in elementary settings, this section might also be useful for teachers of older nonreaders. This is by no means an exhaustive discussion of these elements of reading instruction. However, these sections are included for teachers picking up this book who have vague guidelines for how to proceed with e.i. in reading.

e.i. AND PHONEMIC AWARENESS

Before students are able to decode words, they need to understand that words are made up of individual sounds and can be sounded out (Adams, 1990). Phonemic awareness is knowledge that words are made up of discrete sounds. Without a firm grounding in phonemic awareness skills, students will have difficulty learning phonics later on. As students progress through the elementary grades, weak phonemic awareness and phonics skills become increasingly problematic as students encounter more and more unique words. Students whose difficulties are not identified and corrected are at risk for developing a serious reading deficit (Lyon, 1999).

The research to date strongly supports the notion that explicitly teaching students to manipulate phonemes increases reading and spelling ability (Cunningham, 1990; Davidson & Jenkins, 1994; Lenchner, Gerber, & Routh, 1990). Several instructional principles are recommended for phonemic awareness instruction, such as giving e.i. in blending and segmenting as auditory tasks, particularly at the phoneme level; systematically sequencing phonemic awareness tasks; and using conspicuous strategies that allow students to perceive phonemes. These principles are accomplished through teacher modeling of specific sounds and student production and mental manipulation of specific sounds, often with a concrete representation. This type of instruction has been found to be superior to implicit instruction for helping students apply phonemic awareness skills to the actual task of reading (Cunningham, 1990).

TABLE 8.1	**Instructional Considerations for Phonemic Awareness**
There is a developmental sequence to teaching students to partition words into parts.	First, segmenting a compound word into its two parts (e.g., "What two words are in *cowboy*?")
	Second, segmenting syllables (e.g., "What are the syllables in *likely*?")
	Third, segmenting sounds (e.g., "Let's clap the sounds you hear in *nose*.")
When teaching phonemic awareness, use phoneme sounds, *not* letter names.	/k/, not the letter *k*
Continuant sounds are easier to hear and manipulate than stop consonants.	/m/ is easier to hear than /t/
When identifying sounds in different positions, initial position is easiest, followed by the final position, with the medial position being the most difficult.	First *t*op, then po*t*, then le*tt*er
When identifying or combining sound sequences, the CV (consonant–vowel) pattern should be used before a VC (vowel–consonant) pattern followed by a CVC pattern (consonant–vowel–consonant).	first *pie*, then *egg*, then *red*

Phonemic awareness develops from larger to smaller units. Therefore, certain developmental considerations must be taken into account when sequencing phonemic awareness instruction. For example, identification tasks (e.g., "Which one doesn't rhyme: *cat*, *hat*, or *sun*?") are generally easier than production tasks (e.g., "Tell me the first sound in *car*."). Therefore, if students are having difficulty with a particular phonemic awareness task, you might adjust the difficulty level by changing the response mode from production to identification (e.g., "Find the picture that starts with /r/" will be easier than "What sounds do you hear in *robe*?"). As students develop competence with identification tasks, you can transition to production tasks. Other developmental considerations for phonemic awareness instruction are summarized in Table 8.1.

Phonemic awareness consists of specific skills. Table 8.2 describes e.i. activities that can be used to address each of the phonemic awareness skill areas: rhyme, blending, segmentation, onset and rime, isolated sound recognition, sound deletion, and letter–sound association.

e.i. AND PHONICS

Once students have acquired phonemic awareness skills, reading instruction typically proceeds with e.i. in phonics. Using phonics, or the sounds assigned to letters, is one way students can learn to decode unfamiliar words. Phonics is one of the strategies readers use for words that are not in their sight-word vocabulary. Phonics skills become increasingly important as students enter the intermediate grades and begin to encounter many more unknown words (Chall, 1996). Although the teaching of phonics has been controversial for decades, a body of research-based conclusions about phonics instruction now informs effective practice in this

TABLE 8.2   e.i. in Phonemic Awareness

Phonemic Awareness Skill	Description	Instructional Strategy
Rhyming	The easiest phonemic awareness task, rhyming does not require students to manipulate sounds but does require a certain level of abstraction: in order to be able to tell whether the words *cat* and *hat* rhyme, a student must be able to abstract *-at* from each word, compare them, and note that they are the same. Students who struggle to recognize and create rhyming words may need more direct intervention.	Explicit modeling of examples (e.g., hop—pop; nose—rose) and nonexamples (e.g., car—bed; sun—chair) of rhyming word pairs using pictures. Then present three pictures and ask the student to select and say the two words that rhyme (e.g., "Tell me the two words that rhyme: bus—clock—block."). A variation would be to display two nonrhyming pictures and have the student select the one that rhymes with the word being said by the teacher (e.g., "Here is a *car* and a *fork*. Which picture rhymes with *far*?").
Blending	Sound synthesis, or *blending*, is an essential skill related to later reading ability (Wagner, Torgeson, Laughon, Simmons, & Bashotte, 1993) Blending an initial sound onto the remainder of a word (onset + rime: /m/ + -*an* = *man*)	1. Explicitly model blending an initial sound onto a word, e.g., "It starts with /l/ and ends with /ight/, put it together and it says *light*." Once they have the idea, students supply the final word chorally. As students become proficient, they can take turns presenting their own words to be blended by the class. 2. Using a similar procedure, explicitly model blending syllables of a word together, such as "*Cow* and *boy* form what word?" 3. Proceed to blending isolated phonemes into a word. Model by using a puppet who only says words sound by sound, such as "/d/ /i/ sh/." Students can blend the word individually or chorally.
Segmentation	One of the more difficult phonemic awareness tasks, the act of isolating the sounds in a spoken word by separately pronouncing each one in order. Establishing that sounds occur in different positions of words—initial, final, and medial—helps some students with the later task of segmenting whole words into isolated sound components.	Show students a picture (dog) and ask them to identify the correct word out of three: "Is this a /mmm/-*og*, a /d/d/d/-*og*, or a /sss/-*og*?" Variation: ask if the word has a particular sound: "Is there a /d/ in *dog*?" This can then be switched to "Which sound does dog start with: /d/, /sh/, or /l/?" It is easiest to use continuants that can be

TABLE 8.2   e.i. in Phonemic Awareness *(continued)*

Phonemic Awareness Skill	Description	Instructional Strategy
		exaggerated and prolonged to heighten the sound input (e.g., "/mmmmm/." Iteration should be used with stop consonants to add emphasis (e.g., "/b/ /b/ /b/").
		Several researchers have used visual and tactile cues based on Elkonin boxes to help with phoneme segmentation. A card is prepared with a picture of a simple word at the top. Below the picture is a matrix that contains a box for each phoneme (not letter) in the word. The teacher models the process by slowly articulating the word phoneme by phoneme while pushing a counter into a box for each phoneme. Students can say the word with the teacher while the counters are being placed. Gradually, students should participate with this "say it and move it" activity by placing the counters in each box while saying each sound in a word. Both the matrix and the picture can be eliminated over time so that students are segmenting the word without visual cues.
Onset & rime	Phonograms are the common elements in word families (e.g., the letter sequence -*and* in *sand*, *hand*, *band*, and *land*). The initial consonant that changes the meaning of the word is called he *onset*, and the vowel–consonant combination that remains constant is called the *rime*. Because awareness of syllables, onsets, and rimes develops before an awareness of individual phonemes, the developmental progression of phonemic awareness activities begins with ways to expose students to word families.	Students can make analogies from these syllable units to read and write new words. That is, once a phonogram like -*at* is learned, students can use their knowledge of initial consonants and the -*at* rime to write or read a new word like *sat* or *mat*. Once a student has grasped the more accessible rime units, then the individual phonemes within them are more easily discerned (i.e., "pig" to "ig" to /i/).

TABLE 8.2   e.i. in Phonemic Awareness *(continued)*

Phonemic Awareness Skill	Description	Instructional Strategy
Isolated sound recognition	Students should be familiarized with speech sounds in isolation before they attempt to detect sounds within words. Because students are sometimes unaware that words are made up of individual speech sounds that can be produced in isolation, it is up to the teacher to provide students with a concept of speech sounds.	Associate phonemes with a creature, action, object, or key word that is familiar to the student. For example, the phoneme /s/ can be associated with the hissing sounds a snake makes—/sssssss/. A sound "personality" can also be created (e.g., "Ed" for the short vowel /e/) and introduced in context by selecting a particular sound to talk about that is stressed in poetry or books. Provide pictures that represent sound personalities to promote independence by providing self-correcting cues for students.
Sound deletion	Considered to be more difficult than other types of phonemic awareness tasks, sound deletion activities can be introduced after students exhibit some skill in segmentation and after letter names have been introduced. Because honeme deletion of medial consonants puts an undue burden on young students' memory, sound deletion should target only initial or final sounds in words.	To introduce the idea of deleting parts of a word, the teacher can show pictures or point to objects in the room that are compound words and demonstrate how each word can be said with a part missing. For example, "This is a *hotdog*. If I say *hotdog* without the *hot*, it says *dog*. (Model other examples.) Now you try it. This is a *skateboard*. Say *skateboard* without the *board*." The task of deleting a sound from a word can be made easier by playing a game. The teacher models how to orally segment a word into the "target" sound plus "everything else" and then take the target sound away: "*Chair. It starts with /ch/ and it ends with -air; take the first sound away and it says -air.*" The jingle can be used until students can delete sounds with a less elaborate prompt: "*Say ball without the /b/.*" A sound deletion that results in a "real" word such as *deer* becoming *ear* or *card* becoming *car* is easier than one resulting in a nonsense word such as *book* becoming -*ook*.

TABLE 8.2	e.i. in Phonemic Awareness *(continued)*	
Phonemic Awareness Skill	**Description**	**Instructional Strategy**
Letter-sound correspondence	The most pedagogically sound method of phonemic awareness instruction is one that eventually makes explicit the complete letter-to-sound mappings in segmented words. Phonemic awareness activities that use tokens, blocks, or other visual representations of sounds can be modified to include letter–sound associations.	As individual sounds are mastered by students, their corresponding letter names can be introduced and placed on the tokens (magnetic letters or Scrabble tiles can be used for this) and gradually introduced into segmentation activities. At first, only one letter or token should be provided, and the remainder should be blank. After the student has successfully segmented with one letter or token, others can be added as new letter names are mastered. For example, students select a picture (e.g., *bat*), say the initial sound of the picture (/b/), and identify the letter represented by the first sound by placing the letter *b* in the appropriate box.

TABLE 8.3 Research-Based Conclusions About Phonics Instruction

Phonics instruction can help all students learn to read. Although especially beneficial for those at risk for learning difficulties (i.e., students with learning disabilities, English language learners, and those who enter school with few early literacy experiences), it can also benefit competent readers (Chall, 1967).

Phonics knowledge has a strong effect on decoding ability (Royer & Sinatra, 1994; Stanovich & West, 1989).

Most weak readers have poor phonics skills and rely too much on one strategy (e.g., context clues) (Cunningham, 1995; Stanovich, 1980; Sulzby, 1985).

Phonics instruction should be explicit (Adams, 1990; Anderson et al., 1985; Chall, 1996; Evans & Carr, 1985; Honig, 1995; Stahl & Miller, 1989).

Phonics instruction improves spelling ability (Pinnell et al., 1994).

Teachers' knowledge of phonics affects their ability to teach phonics effectively (Moats, 1995).

Knowledge of syllable types and structural analysis positively affects the ability to spell, read, and learn word meanings (Berninger et al., 2000).

area (see Table 8.3). Contemporary views of phonics instruction suggest that although phonics should not be the sole foundation of a reading program, it should be explicitly taught as one of the strategies readers can use when they want to identify unknown words. For students at risk for learning difficulties or those with reading disabilities, early, systematic, e.i. in phonics is the most beneficial way of helping them become competent readers.

TABLE 8.4   Sample Phonics Scope and Sequence

Consonants *b*, *f*, *m*, *k*, *r*, and *t*

Consonants *p*, *j*, *h*, *s*, *n*, and *d*

Consonants *c*, *l*, *g*, *w*, *y*, *v*, *z*, *q*, and *z*

Short vowels

Initial consonant blends; final consonant blends

One-syllable words ending in a long vowel, including -*y*; silent *e* words, digraphs *sh*, *th*, *wh*, *ch*, -*ng*, -*ck*; trigraph -*tch*; *ee-ea*, *ai-ay*, *oa-ow*

Compound words; common endings -*ful*, -*ing*, -*est*, -*ed*, -*ness*; rules for syllable division between two consonants, with open and closed syllables, with syllables ending in -*y* and -*le*, with vowel and digraph syllables, and with three-syllable words

Word families *all*, *alk*, *old*, *olt*, *oll*, *ild*, *ind*; three letter blends *thr*, *shr*, *scr*, *str*, *spr*, *spl*; *qu* words; -*ey* words; three sounds of -*ed*

Vowel plus r: *ar*, *or*, *er*, *ir*, *ur*, *wor*, *war*; second sound of *ei*; *ie*; *igh*; *oo*; dipthongs *oy-oi* and *ou-ow*; *au-aw*; *ew-ui-ue-ou*

Soft *c* and *g*; silent consonants; *ear*; *ph*; *ei-eigh*

Suffixes and endings

Teachers are sometimes unclear about the order in which phonics instruction should proceed, especially in the absence of a standardized curriculum that includes a phonics scope and sequence. Table 8.4 presents a sample scope and sequence for phonics instruction. It is important to realize, however, that whether or not your school or district adopts a specific phonics program, most students will need at least some e.i. in phonics. Instruction in phonics skills typically proceeds along a developmental continuum of component skills; in other words, as with phonemic awareness skills, phonics skills build one on the next. Table 8.5 presents an instructional model for phonics with suggestions for how phonics instruction can be differentiated across the continuum of mastery. Explicit instruction in phonics is provided at acquisition, followed by skill-based and application-based practice for consolidation and mastery.

Figure 8.2 presents an example of an e.i. lesson in phonics. Because this lesson took place in a first-grade classroom, it is necessarily clear and concise. Several facets of this example provide access to all learners during the e.i. lesson. The teacher uses active participation strategies to engage all learners in the instructional encounter (i.e., signaled response, individual private response, or choral reading). When checking understanding, she prioritizes think time for all students. She also provides a visual or prompt that includes examples and nonexamples of the concept she is trying to teach, thus reducing the memory demand for students with learning difficulties.

e.i. AND VOCABULARY

Students learn new vocabulary in a variety of ways. Most often, they hear and see new words through engaging in daily language activities with peers and adults, being read to by adults, and reading extensively themselves. Research on vocabulary instruction indicates that while most vocabulary is learned indirectly, some vocabulary must be taught directly (Biemiller,

TABLE 8.5   Phonics Instructional Model

Phonics Instructional Model		
Teach (Acquisition)	**Practice (Consolidation)**	**Apply (Mastery)**
1	2	3
Using e.i. to teach phonemic awareness. Literature or poetry can be used to identify the word(s) with the target phonic element in context.	Sort words with picture cards that have both target phonic element and nontarget phonic elements.	Read leveled readers and/or trade books that have words with the target element.
Explicitly teach and model blending consonants and phonograms in the word(s) that contain the target phonic element.	Make words with letter cards.	Have students do a dramatic reading of the story, retell the story, and/or find the words in the story with the target phonic element.
	Use individual pocket charts and letter cards to build words with the target phonic element.	Writing to spell: Have students write original sentences or copy and illustrate sentences from the little books using words with the target phonic element.
	Have students write rhymes using the target phonic element.	Students use hands-on materials, such as a word wheel, to write and illustrate a sentence with words that contain the target phonic element.

2001). Explicit vocabulary instruction includes two components: teaching specific vocabulary and teaching vocabulary learning strategies.

Explicit instruction in specific vocabulary can help expand students' knowledge of word meanings. Increased understanding of word meanings helps students to comprehend what they read and to use words correctly when speaking and writing (Snow, 2002). Research clearly emphasizes that for vocabulary learning to occur, new information must be integrated with what the learner already knows (Stahl & Shiel, 1992). As explained previously, preteaching key vocabulary as a preparatory step to instruction is valuable when readers lack the prior knowledge or background experience to read in a content area such as social studies or science.

Obviously, it is impossible to teach students every new word they might encounter in a text. So how should teachers decide which vocabulary words to teach explicitly? Teachers should focus on teaching a few new words each week following three guidelines:

- Teach words that are important for understanding the text.
- Teach useful words. Instructional time is valuable; use it to teach words that students will encounter and use again and again.
- Teach difficult words. For students with language-based disabilities, words with multiple meanings can be especially challenging to learn. Words that are spelled the same but sound

FIGURE 8.2   What Does e.i. Look Like in Practice? Phonics Lesson.

| Lesson topic: Short vowel /o/ | Subject: Phonics | Grade: 1 |

Learning objective: Students will read and write CVC words with the short vowel /o/ with 100% accuracy.

Align with state curriculum standards:
Standard 3.1.2: Decoding and Word Recognition C.1. Decode regular words and parts of words.

Direct instruction component	Classroom example
Gain students' attention	Boys and girls, I want everyone to get into learning position. Please sit up straight, hands folded, ears open. Is everyone ready?
Inform students of the learning objective	By the end of our phonics lesson today, you will be able to read CVC words with the short vowel sound /o/.
Use informed instruction	This is important to know because if you recognize the CVC pattern, you will be able to use it as a strategy to help you read a lot more words. As I read this story, *Hop on Pop*, by Dr. Seuss, I want you to focus your attention on the story and try to remember one of the words that has the short vowel /o/ sound in it. After we have read the book, we will all be able to compile a list of words that include the short vowel /o/ sound. You will be able to read short *o* words yourselves.
Activate	Let's review the short vowel sounds by singing our vowel song together: "*a* says /a/ /a/; *a* says /a/ /a/; *e* says /e/ /e/; *e* says /e/ /e/; *i* says /i/ /i/; *i* says /i/ /i/; *o* says /o/ /o/; *o* says /o/ /o/; *u* says /u/ /u/; *u* says /u/ /u/; I know my vowels, I know my vowels, AEIOU, AEIOU, I know my vowels I know my vowels."
Cognitive model/ think-aloud	Boys and girls, as I said at the beginning of our lesson, today you are going to learn to read CVC words with the short vowel *o*. First, let's look at the letter *hop*. This is the letter *h*. It is a consonant. This is the letter *o*. It is a short vowel. This is the letter *p*. It is also a consonant. This pattern of letters is called the CVC pattern, for the consonant–vowel–consonant pattern that the letters make. Here is another example: *pop*; *p* is a consonant; *o* is a short vowel; *p* is a consonant. For words that begin and end with one consonant and have a vowel in the middle, the vowel is usually short.
	Boys and girls, here are some other words: *hope, tote, meal*. Give me a thumbs up if you think these are also CVC words. (Students give thumbs down.) That's right. These words have a different letter pattern. They are *not* CVC words.
	Here is a prompt to help you remember this when you come to a CVC word:
	The CVC pattern: For words that begin and end with one consonant and have a medial vowel, the vowel is usually *short*.
	Examples: *mob, log, pot, top, Ron* Nonexamples: *gone, soap, home*

Guided practice	"Boys and girls, on this chart I have a poem called *Tom*. I am going to read it to you, and as I read, if you hear me say a CVC word with *o* or see me point to it on the chart, raise your hand.
	Good, I saw all your hands going up. Now let's read the poem together. (Read chorally.)
	Now let's go back and circle all the CVC words in the poem. First, talk with your partner about the CVC words you see and write them on your whiteboard. Then raise your hand."
Check understanding	"Boys and girls, let's pause for a learning moment. Heads down. When words have the CVC letter pattern, the vowel in the middle is usually WOL1. When you know the answer, raise your thumbs."
Independent practice	Here is a blank big-book page. You are going to write and illustrate your own CVC word with the sound /o/. You can use the procedural prompt or look at the poem chart if you need help.
Closure	"Boys and girls, I am going to hold up a series of cards. Each card has a word written on it. We will read each word together. If you think the word is a CVC word with the /o/ sound, give me a thumbs up. If not, give me a thumbs down. Ready, here we go:
	bun, road, Tom, bin, nod, bog, sun, rob"

different can be difficult (e.g., a *sow* is a female pig; you *sow* seeds in spring) as well as words that sound the same but have different meanings (e.g., you put money in the *bank*; water overflowed the river*bank*). Also difficult for some students are idiomatic expressions such as "drawing a blank" or "get the picture." Such phrases do not mean what their words mean literally; therefore, it is important to explicitly teach students the meanings of such phrases.

An important complement to explicit vocabulary instruction is e.i. in vocabulary learning strategies. Students need strategies to be able to figure out unfamiliar word meanings when they encounter vocabulary that has not been explicitly taught. Vocabulary learning strategies include using dictionaries, glossaries, and thesauruses; using word parts to figure out word meanings (i.e., prefixes, suffixes, base words, and word roots); and using context clues to discover word meanings.

e.i. AND FLUENCY

Fluency is the ability to read text accurately and quickly. When fluent readers read silently, they recognize words automatically and gain meaning from what they read.

Fluent readers read aloud with expression. Their reading sounds effortless and natural, as if they are speaking. Readers who have not developed fluency read laboriously, word by word. Their reading is slow and choppy.

Fluency is important because it provides a bridge to reading comprehension. A recent large-scale study found that of a representative sample of fourth graders, 44% were deficient in fluency (National Assessment of Educational Progress [NAEP], 2007). Students who score low on measures of fluency also tend to score low on reading comprehension. This suggests that fluency is a neglected skill that can negatively affect reading comprehension. Readers who are fluent do not have to expend precious cognitive resources on decoding. As a result, they can focus on what the text means (Wolf & Katzir-Cohen, 2001). In other words, proficient readers are able to fluently decode words and comprehend text at the same time.

Many teachers relay on repeated reading of familiar text to build young readers' fluency. This strategy has been shown to benefit reading fluency, particularly for students who have already acquired decoding skills. However, use of repeated reading in the absence of e.i. in phonics, word recognition, vocabulary, and reading comprehension strategies will not benefit struggling readers (Bowers, 1993; Meyer & Felton, 1999; Wolf & Katzir-Cohen, 2001). In other words, the most effective approach to reading fluency is to provide e.i. in the components of reading in combination with reading opportunities that build accuracy and automaticity.

e.i. AND READING COMPREHENSION

Reading comprehension is the process of constructing meaning from text. Skilled readers are flexible in their use of a variety of strategies for gaining meaning while reading, including summarization, self-questioning, visualization, prediction, and others. Because they constitute an unobservable cognitive process, reading strategies can be difficult to teach and learn. Simply providing opportunities for students to read will not teach most students the strategies they need to become skilled readers. Even though they may have been taught reading strategies, many students will not use them without specific prompting. Therefore, the type of instruction a student receives can dramatically affect his or her reading comprehension ability. Explicit instruction in reading comprehension should begin as students learn to read simple sentences and continue in different forms throughout students' elementary and secondary education. Strategies for improving reading comprehension must be explicitly taught using an approach that includes an expert model of reading comprehension.

Let's consider an example. The QAR (question–answer relationships) strategy (Raphael, 1986) is one that is typically used to help students answer reading comprehension questions. This strategy requires students to classify comprehension questions on the basis of the relationship between the question and the location of its answer. Students are taught that when answering questions, they need to not only consider the text and their prior knowledge but also use strategic behavior to use of each of these sources effectively.

The four types of question–answer relationships (see Table 8.6) are based on the source of information and the types of reasoning involved. First, students are explicitly taught the two major sources of information for answering reading comprehension questions: "in my head" and "in the book." Instruction begins with work on "in the book" responses, then proceeds to those that can be found "in my head." Once students have a clear picture of the difference between "in my head" and "in the book," they are taught the next level of differentiation for each of the major categories. For example, "in my head" responses have two subcategories: whether or not the student needs to read the text for the questions to make sense. Students are taught to identify the type of QAR, the answer to the question, and the strategy they used for finding the answer. Once students can use the QAR strategy with short passages, the teacher can gradually introduce longer passages.

This example illustrates the complexity of providing e.i. in reading comprehension strategies. Each individual component of the QAR strategy must be explicitly taught and modeled by the teacher, and students must be engaged in closely monitored guided practice and prompted to use the strategy independently in diverse settings. The Reading Comprehension Instructional Model presented in Table 8.7 illustrates how comprehension activities can be differentiated across the continuum of mastery. When learning how to provide e.i. in reading comprehension strategies, a common reaction from beginning teachers is, "Ugh, that's too much to remember! These students already have trouble learning. How can I expect them to

TABLE 8.6   The Four Types of Question–Answer Relationships

In the Book	
Right there	Words used to create the question and words used for the answer are in the same sentence.
Think and search	The answer is in the text, but words used to create the question and those used for a correct answer are not in the same sentence.
In My Head	
Author and me	The answer is implied in the author's language, style, and tone.
On my own	The answer is found not in the text but in one's head on the basis of personal experience.

TABLE 8.7   Reading Comprehension Instructional Model

Reading Comprehension Instructional Model		
Teach (Acquisition)	**Practice (Consolidation)**	**Apply (Consultation)**
1	2	3
Develop comprehension using literature for identifying story elements, plot, problem/solution, and so on in context	Guided reading using leveled readers and/or trade books	Literature circles or book discussion groups
Explicitly teach and model reading comprehension strategies using a before–during–after format	Independent reading using leveled books, browsing boxes, or trade books	Retell the story and/or answer reading comprehension questions using the QAR strategy
Teach vocabulary	Build fluency: repeated reading of familiar text	Reading extension activities: Write something about the book Make something about the book Talk about the book

remember all that?" Learning strategies often seem counterintuitive to proficient readers. But to students who struggle to comprehend, e.i. in reading strategies allows them to consistently and automatically do what competent readers do to get the most out of reading.

Instruction in reading strategies is typically organized according to how we would like students to think about applying such strategies. The most commonsense approach to organization, therefore, is according to a before–during–after framework. Before-reading strategies are those that students should use prior to beginning to read a text. Such strategies help prepare students for what the selection might be about, help activate relevant background knowledge, and create a goal or mental set for the reading to follow. During-reading strategies consist of those students should use while they read a text. Such strategies help students make sense of what the author is trying to say and connect it to what they already know about the topic. These strategies also help students self-monitor—attend to whether their attention is focused or has strayed from the reading. After-reading strategies are those that students should use after they have read a text selection. Such strategies are used to reflect on what was read, confirm learning, address lingering questions, and create meaning regarding the author's overall message. Table 8.8 provides a list of before-, during-, and after-reading strategies that can be explicitly taught.

Figure 8.3 presents an example of an e.i. lesson for a reading comprehension strategy. This lesson is designed to teach second graders to identify the main idea of a short expository passage. Although identifying the main idea is an important during- and after-reading strategy, the teacher's preassessment data indicated that 15 out of 19 students were unable to accurately identify the main idea of an expository passage. The main idea strategy taught in this lesson is called *paragraph shrinking* (Fuchs, Mathes, & Fuchs, 1995). In this lesson example, the teacher decided not to use a strategy to prepare students for instruction (e.g., activate background knowledge, preteach key vocabulary, or review). Because learning to identify the main idea is a complex reading comprehension strategy, she chose instead to maximize her instructional time by engaging in expanded cognitive modeling and scaffolded practice using multiple examples. Here, the teacher gives a clear introduction to the lesson while conveying what learning strategies do in meaningful language. Again, the teacher uses active participation strategies throughout the lesson and provides a prompt to help students to remember the steps to the paragraph-shrinking strategy. Cognitive modeling, guided practice, and independent practice are carefully aligned—the procedure modeled by the teacher is exactly the same as what students do during guided and independent practice—to promote students' self-direction in their use of the strategy. A benefit of the e.i. framework is that once you become familiar with its components, you can tailor the degree of structure and control in each lesson to the needs of your learners. The teacher closes the lesson by using a partner strategy to check students' understanding of the paragraph-shrinking procedure.

e.i. AND WRITTEN EXPRESSION

Reading and writing are interrelated, complementary processes (Pinnell, Lyons, DeFord, Bryk, & Seltzer, 1994). Whereas decoding is the process of figuring out the sounds that make up words in print, spelling involves breaking words down into sounds in order to write them correctly. Not surprisingly, research has shown the importance of e.i. in writing (Graham, Harris, & MacArthur, 2006). Explicit writing instruction combined with the writing process is more

TABLE 8.8   Reading Strategies for Explicit Instruction

Before-reading strategies	Preview headings, picture walk, reading introductions and summaries, prediction, and K-W-L
During-reading strategies	Self-questioning, prediction, visualization, paraphrasing, elaboration (comparing what is read to what is known), and rereading
	Students should be using what was done before reading to help their understanding during reading
After-reading strategies	Summarization, providing a postorganizer, completing a study guide of what was learned, verifying predictions, and after-reading self-questioning
	RAP:
	Read a paragraph
	Ask yourself what the paragraph was about
	Put the main idea and two supporting details in your own words
	Main idea
	Summarization
	1. Explain and show
	2. Find the main idea
	3. Select or create a topic sentence
	4. Select details
	5. Paraphrase and condense:
	a. Collapse details into a more general statement, e.g.,
	i. Maria read her science chapter, answered the questions at the end, read 20 pages, and worked on her social studies project.
	ii. Maria did her homework.
	6. Compare
	7. Check for clarity
	Provide frames for summaries:
	Topic sentence: The Phoenicians worked at many different trades and occupations.
	1.
	2.
	3.
	4.

effective than the writing process alone. The most effective writing instruction involves high input from both students and teachers. The least effective are classrooms in which teacher input is high and student input is low, in other words, those in which teachers use a traditional approach and provide students with few authentic opportunities to apply their writing skills (Pressley, Mohan, Fingeret, Reffitt, & Bogaert, 2007).

Written expression typically refers to skills in handwriting, spelling, and composition. At some point in their development, most students can benefit from e.i. in these areas. For students

FIGURE 8.3   What Does e.i. Look Like in Practice? Reading Comprehension Lesson.

Lesson topic: Main idea   Subject: Reading comprehension   Grade: 2

Learning objective: Students will identify the main idea of a three- or four-sentence passage for one of one trial.

Align with state curriculum standards:
Standard 2: Construct, examine, and extend the meaning of literary, informative, and technical texts.
2.4d: Demonstrate an overall understanding of printed texts by (d) retelling a story or restating an informative text through speaking and/or writing.
Grade 2 expectations: Retell/restate the main idea of a simple informative text with supporting details.

Direct instruction component	Classroom example
Gain students' attention	Students have gathered on the carpet. The teacher introduces the lesson by asking, "What super power would you like to have?" Briefly (2 to 3 minutes) discuss super powers that could help students learn. Explain that being able to shrink objects would be a great way to learn and remember the most important information about what we read.
Inform students of the learning objective	Today you are going to learn to ask some specific questions about the most important thing you read. This is called the main idea.
Use informed instruction	Finding the main idea will make you better readers because it will help you learn what's most important to remember. We can't remember everything we read, but we want to remember what's most important. This strategy is called *paragraph shrinking*. It's a way to pick the most important thing to remember while you are reading. It is our super power for reading.
Activate prior knowledge	Not applicable.
Cognitive model/ think-aloud	When a reader uses the paragraph-shrinking strategy, first she reads, then she stops and names the *who* or the *what* that the text is about. Then she tells the most important thing about the *who* or the *what*. Next, she states the main idea. To make sure it's clear, the main idea should be a sentence with 10 or fewer words. This helps her figure out what is most important. These steps are written on this prompt card (posted on the blackboard): 1. Read 2. Identify who or what 3. Say the most important thing (main idea) you read about the *who* or the *what* 4. Say it in 10 or fewer words Now I am going to show you how to use this strategy. First, I am going to read this paragraph (written on a flip chart) and think about the *who* or the *what*:

The tropical forests of the world are lush green wonderlands. The trees there grow hundreds of feet high. Smaller trees and shrubs cover the ground. Thick rain-forest vines wind around tree trunks and branches and hand like long ropes. Colorful orchids and other flowers add to the forests' beauty.

I am going to circle the word or words for the *who* or the *what*. In this case, the *what* is *tropical forests*.

Next, I am going to tell the most important thing about the *what*. I am going to circle the most important idea about tropical forests in the text I just read. The most important idea is that *there are many green plants*.

Finally, I will say the main idea in 10 or fewer words: "Tropical forests have many green plants." That's six words.

Now, I'm going to model the strategy again with another example. I will let you know what I'm thinking as I read:

The tropical rain forest is one kind of tropical forest. This rich green area receives a huge amount of rainfall all year-round. There are also seasonal tropical forests. These regions have a dry season as well as a wet season. Seasonal tropical forests do not have as many different kinds of trees and plans as rain forests do.

Let me think . . . what's the first step in paragraph shrinking? Let me check the prompt card. I need to read, stop, and think about the *who/what*. I am going to circle the *who/what* in the passage. My *who* or *what* is about tropical rain forests, so I'm circling the words *tropical forest* in the text. Now let me think . . . what is the next step in paragraph shrinking? I need to think about the most important thing about the *what* (tropical forests). I am underlining the most important thing in the passage: *there are two different types of tropical forests—tropical rain forests and seasonal tropical forests—and they each get different amounts of rain.* Okay, what's the last step? I need to tell the main idea in 10 or fewer words. I am going to write my main idea: *There are two different types of tropical forests.* I will count up the words. That's eight words.

Guided practice

"Now, let's try one together. What's the first step? Everyone responds, *Read the passage.* Let's read it together:

All tropical forests have a wide variety of animals. However, inch for inch, they contain more life than any other region on earth. Many tropical forest plants and animals cannot be found anywhere else.

What's the next step? Think about the *who/what* and circle it. What do I do now? Think about what's the most important thing about the *who/what* and underline it. What do I do last? Write your main idea on the line. Then count up your words to see how many words are in your main idea. Are there 10 or fewer words? Discuss and provide corrective feedback.

(continued)

Check understanding	Turn to the person next to you and tell them the four steps to paragraph shrinking. Then raise your hand.
Independent practice	"Now you are going to try paragraph shrinking on your own. Use the prompt card to help you remember the steps."
	Students engage in independent practice using two different paragraphs.
Closure	Today we learned the paragraph-shrinking strategy. On your index card, please write the four steps to the paragraph-shrinking strategy. Trade with the person next to you and check. Make any necessary corrections and hand your card to me.

with learning difficulties, one or all of these may be problematic, creating a significant barrier to effective written communication.

e.i. AND HANDWRITING

Competent handwriting is a functional necessity for students at all levels. Many teachers reason that this is no longer the case since most people now use computers for writing. Computers are effective alternatives for students who have great difficulty with handwriting. However, it is important to recognize that weak fine motor skills alone do not account for difficulties with handwriting. Writing is a written language process; as with reading, fluency is important. If students fail to develop handwriting fluency, it could be sign of a more significant learning problem.

Once students have been introduced to letter formation, they must learn to retrieve and produce letters automatically. Forming letters from memory can present handwriting problems for some students. Handwriting fluency, which is assessed by the number of letters written correctly within a brief period of time, is a strong predictor of the quality of composition in normally developing and disabled writers (Graham, Berninger, Abbott, Abbott, & Whitaker, 1997). If letter production is automatic, memory space is freed up for higher-level composition processes, such as deciding what to write about, what to say, and how to say it. Thus, students who do not acquire fluency with the mechanical aspects of writing will have difficulty composing written work.

Research on handwriting suggests that handwriting problems are greatest among students who have academic difficulties. Illegible, dysfluent, laborious writing interferes with students' abilities to complete written assignments in a timely fashion, take notes in class, read and study notes they have written, and undertake writing tasks. Illegibly written assignments receive lower grades and receive less careful consideration by teachers. Explicit instruction in handwriting emphasizes the skills and strategies presented in Table 8.9.

TABLE 8.9   Handwriting Skills and Strategies
Uses appropriate paper and equipment (e.g., paper with more space between lines, raised lines, or color-coded lines and adaptive pencil grips)
Explicitly models the order, number, and direction of strokes
Provides sufficient practice tracing, copying, and writing from memory
Uses behavioral techniques such as cuing, shaping, and positive reinforcement
Teaches self-regulation behaviors such as self-verbalization during tracing, copying, and writing from memory
Incorporates self-instruction, self-correction, and self-assessment as part of handwriting instruction

e.i. AND SPELLING

Spelling is part of both reading and writing instruction. Efficient spelling relies on many of the same skills as proficient reading: good memory, phonemic awareness, orthographic skills, phonics skills, sight vocabulary, and self-checking skills. These are often deficit areas for students with learning difficulties. Thus, spelling can be a complex and difficult task for students with reading and writing problems. As with vocabulary instruction, explicit spelling instruction includes teaching specific words as well as teaching students strategies for becoming independent spellers (Graham, 1999).

First, consideration must be given what spelling words will be explicitly taught. In order for students to become proficient spellers, teachers should provide e.i. in decoding and spelling that emphasizes letter–sound correspondences. For students with learning difficulties, approaches that group words according to their common spelling patterns (e.g., phonograms) are most effective. Words can also be selected from reading and writing activities. Spelling words that are relevant can also be easier to learn because students can apply the decoding skills they are learning in reading to spelling. Students may also be more likely to see the importance of learning to spell these words as compared to random words on a list.

There are additional considerations if students receive a weekly list of spelling words. First, be certain that they can actually read all the words on their list. This may seem like a silly recommendation, but lists are sometimes distributed (e.g., as homework) without a thorough check that all students can read the words. If students cannot decode the words, they will certainly have difficulty learning to spell them. Lists of spelling words can also be shortened to accommodate students with spelling problems. Differentiated spelling curricula provide students in the same class with modified word lists (e.g., students with disabilities to learn five rather than 10 words per week). Shorter lists can improve spelling performance on weekly tests. However, shortened lists will not help if the words themselves are beyond students' current abilities.

Recommendations regarding spelling instruction for students with spelling difficulties include introducing a small number of words daily (rather than providing a large list all at once) and providing distributed practice activities over time. Shorter, more frequent periods for studying rather than fewer, longer periods are more beneficial (e.g., several 15 minutes spelling activities scheduled throughout the school day could reinforce learning better than one 45-minute block). Peer tutoring sessions can also help students with special needs. After training students in peer tutoring procedures, peer tutoring can provide students with extra opportunities to practice spelling new words. Flash cards can be used and students can record or graph their daily performance.

Students should also be taught strategies for more efficient independent spelling. Mnemonic strategies can help students to remember the difficult or unpredictable parts of words, such as the *s* in "island." These can be created by having students think of a sentence that contains the difficult word and another, smaller word that includes the most difficult part of the word (e.g., Don't *mar* your writing with bad gram*mar*; You *gain* when you buy a bar*gain*; or A princi*pal* is your *pal*). Some students will also need to be explicitly taught how to study spelling words (e.g., say the word, look at the model, and study the spelling; then cover the model and try to copy the word from memory; finally, look at the model and compare their spelling with the model). Often, we just assume that students know how to study when this is not the case. Finally, students can be explicitly taught skills to compensate for poor spelling. These include how to use the dictionary, computer spell check, and electronic spellers.

e.i. AND COMPOSITION

Written composition is a sophisticated level of communication that requires the integration of language, spelling, and reading skills. Less research exists on instruction for composition than for spelling and handwriting, and the extant research contradicts commonly accepted wisdom regarding how composition skills can best be taught. For example, although some teachers believe strongly in its merits, traditional rule-based grammar instruction actually has little effect on the quality of student writing (Saddler & Graham, 2005).

Proficient writers have sophisticated strategies for how they approach writing tasks and evaluate their own writing performance. Struggling writers, on the other hand, do not approach writing tasks strategically. They do not make revisions beyond simple corrections, equating a good paper with one that is devoid of spelling errors. Poor writers typically lack awareness of text structure (genres), the fact that the writing process involves recursive planning, sentence generation and revising, their own cognitive processes in writing, or areas in which they need improvement.

Research on proficient writers' cognitive processes has led to the development of writing strategies designed to promote better writing. Three writing strategies that are supported by research include sentence-combining (Saddler, 2005; Saddler & Graham, 2005), sentence expansion (Christensen, 1963, 1965), and paragraph-based strategies (Graham & Harris, 2005). Sentence combining teaches students to combine several shorter sentences into longer, more elaborate sentences. Sentence expansion begins with a "sentence kernel" (e.g., Sally jumped) and teaches students to integrate more details based on *who, what, when, where, and why*. For example, students can be taught to use action words, action helper words (adverbs), and describing words as they write. Paragraph-based methods teach students sentence patterns within paragraph types. For example, students learn to write a topic sentence, supporting details, and conclusion sentence for a persuasive paragraph.

In addition to teaching strategies for improving written products, it can also be important to explicitly teach affective strategies that improve how students approach writing tasks. Many students abandon writing assignments because they are overwhelmed with the mechanical obstacles of handwriting, spelling, and punctuation. Self-regulation and self-instructional strategies help students develop planning, self-correction, and self-regulation skills (e.g., imparting structure to open-ended writing tasks and reinforcing themselves for their attention

TABLE 8.10   Self-Regulation and Self-Instructional Strategies for Writing

Strategy	Description
Problem definition	Identify the nature and demands of the task: What do I have to do? What is the first step?
Attention and planning	Think of the steps and make a plan: First, I need to . . .
Self-evaluation and error correction	Have I used all the story parts? I missed one—I can revise. Am I following my plan?
Coping and self-control	Don't worry; worry doesn't help. I can handle this . . . I need to go slow and take my time . . .
Self-reinforcement	Providing self-reward: I'm getting better at this; I like this ending; I'm done!

and effort) (Graham, 2006). Such skills may improve the writing performance of students who are easily frustrated by the demands of writing tasks. A list of self-regulation and self-instructional strategies for writing (Graham & Harris, 2005) is presented in Table 8.10.

Meaningful guided practice for writing involves students in the writing process by having them choose their own topics, write daily, and revise their products in collaboration with teachers and peers. These activities help reinforce the idea that writing is communication to an audience and that peers can be helpful in expanding and improving writing skills.

Summary

This chapter discussed the importance of high-quality e.i. in literacy in the general education classroom from the beginning of the school years. When schools provide ineffective literacy instruction in the primary grades and stop the teaching of reading after the third grade, many students are left to flounder as they struggle with increasingly advanced reading and writing requirements. Early reading failure exacts a tremendous toll on students' later school performance; approximately two-thirds of the nation's high school students read below grade level (NAEP, 2007). Key skills central to reading development were highlighted in the context of e.i., including phonemic awareness, phonics, fluency, vocabulary, and comprehension. The role of e.i. in writing instruction was also presented.

CHAPTER 9

Explicit Instruction in the Content Areas

The previous chapter discussed explicit instruction (e.i.) as a method for improving student literacy. Strong literacy skills are important for understanding academic content, communicating effectively, and participating in the larger community. Building student literacy, therefore, addresses issues of inclusivity and access for all students. The standards movement has emphasized that all students should understand content on a deeper, more elaborative level than has been advocated previously for anyone but highly advanced students. Many content area learners will have difficulty constructing meaning and deriving usefulness from what they learn because of either underdeveloped literacy skills or content area teaching that fails to meet their needs. This chapter discusses how e.i. can be applied in mathematics and the content areas (e.g., social studies, science, history, and English).

e.i. AND MATHEMATICS

In recent years, school reform efforts and federal policy mandates have drawn increased attention to the issue of how best to teach mathematics. As with reading, many students need e.i. in order to learn math (Montague, 1998). Research findings and the results of several meta-analyses (Ellis, 1993; Karp & Voltz, 2000; Swanson, 2001) indicate that a combination of e.i. and strategy instruction in math has a greater effect than either method alone. In other words, using e.i. to teach skills and strategies that help students store and retrieve information they have learned produces the most positive effect on math achievement. These approaches are particularly critical for students who are at risk or have math disabilities.

Current thinking in math instruction emphasizes active, self-regulated, and self-directed construction of mathematical knowledge, including functional skill acquisition as well as creative thinking and conceptual understanding of math (Montague, 1997). Math reform curricula often emphasize a spiral curriculum—in other words, rather than focusing on the same concept for a few days or weeks until it is mastered, several mathematical concepts are integrated into a single lesson. While these kinds of instructional strategies reflect what research has shown about the development of mathematical reasoning, it is important to recognize that, for a variety of reasons, not all students are at a point where they are able to actively and independently solve problems or articulate their reasoning—either because of a lack of math knowledge or because of language-based disabilities (Mercer, Lane, Jordan, Allsopp, & Eisele, 1996; Miller & Mercer, 1997). Innovative curricula and pedagogy may be necessary and sufficient to have a positive impact on average- and high-achieving learners; however, they may be insufficient for students with learning difficulties in math (Woodward & Baxter, 1997). In such cases, it is necessary to deliver math instruction that meets students' needs for successful skill acquisition in both computation and problem solving. Pressley and McCormick (1995) recommended explicit teaching in the context of multicomponent instruction for helping students with math difficulties become proficient problem solvers. Mercer, Jordan, and Miller (1996) suggested a continuum of explicit to implicit instruction in math by describing the degree and intensity of teacher assistance, the level of student independence, and the typical content that characterizes each type of instruction. Addressing the needs of the diverse population of students in mathematics classrooms, therefore, involves using a variety of approaches, techniques, and strategies, including e.i. for students who need it (Montague, 1998).

Explicit instruction variables that are particularly meaningful to mathematics instruction include daily and ongoing reviews, presentation and explanation of new material related to both skill and strategy development, modeling, scaffolded guided practice, and independent practice (Silbert, Stein, & Carnine, 1997). Students with disabilities, in particular, may not naturally draw connections between previously learned skills or concepts and the lesson about to be taught. In order to facilitate explicit connections between component skills, e.i. in math should include daily reviews of content covered in the previous lessons. For example, before teaching a lesson on skip counting by twos, a first-grade teacher might lead students in a review of counting by ones, pointing to each number on the number line as students count aloud. If homework had been assigned on this topic, this would be an appropriate time to check students' performance for understanding.

In addition to daily reviews, weekly and monthly reviews are especially valuable in math. In special education or inclusive settings, many students may need additional practice with newly introduced skills in order to become fluent to the point of overlearning. In the absence of frequent, ongoing, and meaningful reviews, many students fail to master basic math skills, making subsequent learning more difficult. Reviews help to ensure long-term retention and allow for easier application and generalization of newly acquired skills. Review sessions can be optimal times for implementing peer learning strategies (e.g., think–pair–share and do–check–teach). Reviews can also document progress toward mastery of goals and objectives of individualized education plans. At these times, students can also be informed of their progress.

As with other e.i. lessons, presentation of new information in math begins with clarification of the goals and objectives for the day's lesson. The teacher presents several examples in step-by-step fashion using a "model–lead–test" approach (i.e., I model, we do it together, then you try it). Explicit instruction in math, as in other content areas, involves the teacher in providing instruction in an explicit, step-by-step manner. During modeling, the teacher tells students the procedures to use and simultaneously presents an example. For example, when teaching the addition of decimals, the teacher would begin with a review of adding integers. He or she would be careful to highlight important steps (e.g., lining up each column before you add) or prerequisite knowledge (e.g., the meaning of the decimal point). The teacher would demonstrate how the decimals need to be lined up and model problems that require the addition of decimals several times, verbally guiding her way through each problem. At this stage, the teacher might introduce a procedural prompt and integrate its use into the modeling procedure.

Remediation of computation problems in students with learning disabilities (LD) often consists of designing effective prompts to ease memory load in students with LD. In math computation, each problem typically has a set of steps that might be scripted (e.g., on a prompt card; see Table 9.1) to promote student accuracy and reduce demands on memory. For example, for a student with LD who has just been taught the computational procedure of adding decimals, you might use a large index card on which the computational procedure is shown step-by-step in one column. An adjacent column shows verbal statements correspon-ding to each computational step. Computational steps should come from the same demon-stration example used *in the teacher's e.i.* In other words, on the *same* side of this large index card, the student with LD sees the decimal addition problem that the teacher just explained and taught him, each computational step clearly laid out, and the accompanying verbal state-ments in the adjacent column. The student can refer to this prompt card whenever he needs to as he calculates decimal addition both in school and during homework.

Next, the teacher presents another example and leads students through the procedure by asking guided questions that promote self-regulation (e.g., What do we do first? What's the next step? What do we do last? How should we self-check?). Another example should then be provided. This format should be followed until it is determined that students are ready for a guided practice activity. In other words, the teacher provides as many examples and as much support as necessary in order to move students toward independent practice.

Once students are ready for guided and independent practice, a key consideration is that practice activities are directly related to the lesson's main objective. When students have learned the new skill and are performing it accurately with guidance, the teacher can then pro-ceed to independent practice. In math, independent practice often consists of pencil-and-paper tasks that students are required to complete on their own. Problems can be created when teachers simply release students to engage in independent practice without monitoring their work. During this stage, quick and accurate performance needs to be reinforced. Therefore, it is critical for teachers to initially guide and closely monitor students during inde-pendent practice. For example, once the independent practice activity has been explained, the teacher should lead students through the first few examples to ensure that they understand the task. Once students begin independent work, the teacher can make a quick sweep around

TABLE 9.1   Prompt Card for Addition of Decimals

Addition of Decimals	
11.4 + 5.1	
11.4 5.1	1. Write 11.4, 2. Write 5.1 underneath. Remember to line up the decimals!
11.4 + 5.1 ——	3. Bring the decimal point straight down into your answer.
11.4 + 5.1 —— 16.5	4. Add the numbers. 5. Check your answer.

the classroom to pinpoint students who are having difficulty. These students can then be taken aside for further help or reteaching.

After modeling several examples like this, the teacher would allow students to practice a variety of addition problems, some involving skills the students have already mastered (by way of review) and some involving the new skill. When students have achieved mastery (as determined through ongoing progress monitoring), the teacher would move on to the next skill but continue to review and reinforce addition of decimals.

Figure 9.1 presents an example of e.i. in secondary math. This example illustrates how e.i. can be used effectively in secondary math for students who need more structured explication of mathematical concepts. As discussed previously, e.i. would be used in combination with a variety of other approaches as part of multicomponent mathematics instruction. The teacher's instruction of new concepts progresses in a natural way from least complex to most complex. Although this is a secondary classroom, the teacher still promotes active participation and accountability by using e.i. in combination with peer learning strategies to promote active engagement. He also increases active participation by providing a prompt for students who may need a reduced memory burden during math reasoning.

FIGURE 9.1   What Does e.i. Look Like in Practice? Secondary Algebra Lesson.

Lesson topic: Polynomials   **Subject: Algebra**   **Grade: 9**

Learning objective: Students will write an example of each of the three kinds of polynomials (monomial, binomial, and trinomial) with 100% accuracy.

Align with state curriculum standards:
NJCCCS Standard 4.2

Direct instruction component	Classroom example
Gain students' attention	"Good afternoon, class. Thank you for giving me your attention to promptly."
Inform students of the learning objective	"Today you are going to learn about polynomials and how to identify each of the different types."
Use informed instruction	"We are still talking about polynomials but in more detail. The lesson topic and agenda are written on the board. Here is our agenda for today's lesson: 1. Review and collect homework 2. Lesson on polynomials 3. Work in pairs on models 4. Worksheet"
Review previously learned skills	The teacher leads a brief, explicit (step-by-step) review of the homework. The initial problems are reviewed in more detail. For later problems the teacher will step away and solicit student answers. Students ask questions about difficult problems, such as 6 (−2) (3)/2.

Cognitive model/think-aloud	The teacher presents the lesson in small steps using the model–lead–test approach and varied examples and nonexamples: 1. Model a monomial and give multiple examples on copied notes. Explain "mono"—mono/stereo sound sources; "mono" means "one." 2. Guided practice with monomial. 3. Show students a binomial. "This is called a binomial. A binomial is a polynomial that has two terms. Note that all binomials have either a plus or a minus sign between the two terms. We can use this plus or minus to identify a binomial" (for "bi-," explain using "bi-cycle"). Show multiple examples. 4. Guided practice with binomial. 5. Show students a trinomial. "This is called a trinomial. A trinomial is a polynomial that has three terms. Note that all trinomials have *two* plus or minus signs between the three terms." (for "tri-," explain using "tri-cycle"). 6. Guided practice with trinomial.
Guided practice	Do a basic summary of the three types of polynomials and then supply students with a mix of polynomials and have students identify just one of the polynomials at a time (e.g., "Identify all of the monomials."). The same mixed set of polynomials can be used for each: monomials, binomials, and trinomials. Students are closely guided, and every answer is checked so as not to let inaccurate ideas take hold. The teacher provides a procedural prompt for students who confuse terms: Monomial: a polynomial with one term (e.g., $5x$) Binomial: a polynomial with two terms (e.g., $5x - 10$) * Contains one plus or minus sign Trinomial: a polynomial with three terms (e.g., $7x^4 - 6x^2 + 5$) * Contains two plus or minus signs
Check understanding	The teacher asks specific questions to check understanding: * "$5a + 5b$. Why is this not an example of one quantity?" * "In this classroom we have seven boys and eight girls. Think of an example of a polynomial that illustrates this quantity." Students use think–pair–share to discuss their answers. The teacher provides positive and corrective feedback. In their pairs, students generate their own examples (such as the boys and girls example) for monomials, binomials, and trinomials.

(continued)

| Independent practice | Students write three different examples of each kind of polynomial as the teacher circulates around the classroom to monitor performance. |
| Closure | The teacher hands out index cards. "On the index card, write how you know if a polynomial is a monomial, binomial, or trinomial. Then write one question you have about polynomials. Hand me your card on the way out." (Bell rings; students hand the teacher their index cards and leave the classroom.) |

e.i. IN THE CONTENT AREAS

Explicit instruction in the content areas most often involves teaching students strategies for *how to learn*. Research-based recommendations for teaching learning strategies include elements of e.i. such as modeling, guided practice, and feedback (Deshler & Schumaker, 1988). In particular, strategy instruction has been found to be a key component for helping adolescents with learning problems manage the vast amount of content required in secondary school.

Reading, writing, spelling, and test taking are among memory's biggest consumers in school. This is because students are required to consistently and competently perform these skills across all the content areas. As content demands increase across the school years, content area learning can be a mounting struggle for many students. Research indicates that students who are at risk or have LD often have difficulty with encoding, storage, and retrieval of new content, skills, and strategies (Torgesen, 1985). Their storage problems reflect strategic deficiencies; apparently, such students are unaware that they should approach learning in a planful and strategic manner. Storage problems also result from insufficient background knowledge with which to integrate or anchor new learning. These processes are interdependent; in other words, retrieval problems can be confounded by storage problems or even encoding problems.

The assumption that students with learning problems completely lack metacognitive skills is invalid. Rather, their metacognitive skills are qualitatively different (not absent or developmentally delayed) from those of their normally achieving peers (Wong, 1986). For example, through daily struggles with math computation, some students develop the misguided strategy that when they encounter a difficult problem, they should spend more time studying it and puzzling over it. However, more time will not benefit a student who does not have a *useful* strategy for how to approach the problem. Mastery of basic math skills and flexible problem-solving strategies is the appropriate path to success for such students.

As students advance through the grade levels, they are required to see many more teachers throughout the school day, to manage many more books and materials, to master varying and often confusing class schedules, and to plan for short-term and long-range homework assignments. In addition, they might have extracurricular activities, a part-time job, and responsibilities at home to consider. Some teachers object to the idea of having to spend instructional time structuring certain students. Particularly after they reach a certain age, students should "just know" how to study and organize themselves. On the surface, it makes sense that a teacher might be frustrated at having to teach a high school student how to organize a notebook or binder. This frustration is often based on the assumption that the student already *has* the skills to be organized and successful but chooses to be lazy or sloppy. This is a dangerous assumption (all of us know disorganized adults who probably never mastered such skills) and one that can exact a deep cost in students' performance. Students with disabilities, low-achieving students, and others have poorly developed organization and study skills and learning strategies. Explicit instruction in study skills and learning strategies is required before such students can become self-regulated and self-directed studiers.

e.i. AND STUDY SKILLS

Study skills that can be explicitly taught include personal organization skills (e.g., how to clean out a desk or locker, binder organization, and how to use an assignment notebook), strategies for homework, test taking, and note taking.

Personal organization skills (also called *self-management skills*) help students structure themselves so that they can become independent, self-directed learners. Many students depend on their teachers or parents to impart structure on schoolwork and study time. However, when adults continue to play this role, it virtually guarantees that the student will remain dependent throughout his or her school years. Understandably, parents and teachers reach a point where they become fatigued at having to play this role; work demands increase over time, students become increasingly frustrated and resentful at being dependent, and teachers and parents don't have unlimited time to devote to certain individuals. Over time, conflict ensues. At that point, the exasperated adults usually decide that it's time for the student to "shape up" and "sink or swim." He or she will most certainly sink if not explicitly taught effective strategies for self-directed learning.

Personal organization skills include the following:

- Using time schedules and time management
- Understanding class and school schedules
- Using a planner for short-term and long-range planning
- Being organized for completing homework assignments (e.g., looking in your assignment book, deciding what materials are needed, and transferring all needed materials from locker to backpack)
- Analyzing task demands (e.g., break a large task down into component steps, estimate time for each step, and write out what needs to be done, sequence the steps, estimate time for each step)

Some students will need explicit step-by-step teaching, scaffolded practice, and reinforcement of each of these procedures. Notice the difference between saying to a disorganized student, "You need an assignment notebook!" and using a sample planner to provide explicit thinking in each of these steps: look in your planner, prioritize your tasks, set goals for finishing individual tasks, write each step in your planner, persevere at completing identified goals, and reinforce yourself for a job well done. After e.i. and practice, reinforce students when their work is completed on time because of good planning. Students are not likely to repeat good study skills when adults react with sarcasm (e.g., "Your work is in on time—that's a first!").

Homework is another area in which task demands increase substantially as students ascend through the grade levels. The intention behind homework is that it develops fluency with skills, strategies, and content acquired during the school day; in essence, it is a form of extended practice. Many teachers struggle with students' homework completion. Once again, before blaming poor homework completion on laziness or apathy, it is important to analyze whether students have the skills to successfully complete homework. Is it possible that they just can't remember what went on in class? Are their notes insufficient or illegible? Do they even think to take their homework out of their backpack and look at it? If they do look at it, do they quickly decide it's too difficult and abandon the task? Is there an incentive (either intrinsic or extrinsic) for homework completion?

As with personal organization skills, many students need e.i. and structured support in order to complete homework effectively. Homework strategies can be easily integrated into e.i. lessons as part of review or closure activities. Incorporating homework into e.i. provides students with the expectation that homework will be explained, distributed, and collected at the same time each day. This cuts down on the chances that students will "miss" homework assignments. Similarly, write or post homework assignments in the same place every day and provide a few minutes of class time for students to write in their planners. As part of homework assignments, articulate the materials that students will need in order to complete the homework. During class time, explicitly teach and repeat the instructions as needed, completing the first few questions or examples together so that students have a model at home.

Most successful learners study, at least in part, using class notes. Many students—not just those with learning difficulties—are never taught effective note-taking strategies. As a result, they often end up with insufficient, poorly organized notes. Some students believe that taking copious notes is what makes a good student; however, these students often fail to meaningfully comprehend much of what went on in class because of their incessant writing. In actuality, good note takers do not write down every word verbatim. They summarize key points and develop shorthand abbreviations so they don't have to write entire sentences. This frees up the majority of their attention and effort for processing classroom instruction.

Most students need to be explicitly taught note-taking skills and strategies. Beginning this instruction when students are young gives them the opportunity to develop their own individual style of note taking over time. Use examples and nonexamples to explicitly teach the characteristics of good notes (e.g., each new lecture and page is dated, legible, and organized and uses summarization and/or shorthand abbreviations). Once students begin to approximate satisfactory notes, begin to explicitly teach students how to study using their notes (e.g., review notes frequently, make note of questions/points of clarification, use highlighters to identify key points, and use sticky notes to attach questions where they arise). Not all students will use every strategy that you teach. Rather, help students articulate what works for them and reinforce them for developing their own useful note-taking/studying system.

In some cases, students may have difficulties that prevent them from being able to take their own notes. In such cases, you can provide note-taking adaptations, such as formats for note taking (e.g., a blank outline or graphic organizer with major headings filled in) or guided notes (e.g., cloze notes with blanks where students fill in important terms as they arise in class). In fact, you may want to vary the use of these adaptations regularly for all students in the class. Note-taking formats can provide scaffolds for students as they begin to learn how to take their own notes. Cloze notes are especially useful when you want students to really look and listen rather than spend class time bent over their notebooks (e.g., during a demonstration or when watching an instructional video). Experiences with different types of note taking can help students learn what works best for them.

e.i. AND LEARNING STRATEGIES

Most self-directed learners have a set of strategies for how they learn best. These may involve the use of visuals or graphic organizers, extended periods of reading and review, making lists, studying with a partner, or a combination of these. Competent learners consistently evaluate their own performance and make adjustments to their strategies accordingly. They want to be able to answer the question, "How well am I doing with this?"

The power of learning strategies is they require students to *elaborate*. Elaboration refers to deliberately forming mental relationships between new information and prior knowledge (e.g., by evoking mental images, using verbal elaborations, or summarizing or paraphrasing text). The purpose of elaborative techniques is to make information more understandable or memorable. For example, students may attempt to picture in their minds what is occurring in a story (use mental imagery), try to put the author's ideas into their own words (paraphrase), or try to relate them to their own experiences (personalize).

Learning strategies can be task based or metacognitive. Task-based learning strategies help students complete specific tasks through the use of resources or the provision of structure. Task-based strategies include predicting, using background knowledge, inference, paraphrasing, and the use of mnemonics, key words, and acronyms. Task-based strategies can also include breaking previously overwhelming tasks down into manageable parts (e.g., "write a persuasive essay" becomes a series of incremental steps). Metacognitive strategies are those that teach students how to *think* about their thinking. Most metacognitive strategies follow a before–during–after format and help students plan, manage, monitor, and evaluate their own learning.

Researchers have developed specific strategies for content area learning. The Strategic Instruction Model (SIM; Deshler, Ellis, & Lenz, 1996), for example, is a collection of interventions designed to help students learn how to learn and to help teachers teach more effectively. A key finding in the implementation of the SIM strategies is the extent to which student performance changes when e.i. is used to teach the strategies (Schumaker & Deshler, 1992). In order for learning strategies to be acquired, mastered, and generalized, students must be explicitly taught to use them.

Learning strategies that can be explicitly taught include the following:

- Reading strategies (summarization, paraphrasing, word identification, self-questioning, and visualization)
- Studying and remembering (mnemonics, paired associates, and LINCS vocabulary strategy)
- Writing (sentence writing, paragraph writing, theme writing, error monitoring, and editing)
- Assignment completion and test taking (multiple-choice strategies, essay-writing strategies, and task analysis)
- Self-advocacy
- Social skills, class participation, and cooperation

Summary

Students are required to read and write extensively in the content areas. This can be a challenge for students who never finished learning how to read and write proficiently. Historically, content area instructors have been reluctant to provide e.i. in reading, writing, or learning strategies. Most content area teachers spend little class time teaching students what it means to be a good reader and writer in a given content area (Wade & Moje, 2000). The reasons for this are easily intuited: most middle and secondary teachers consider themselves content area specialists, not basic skills instructors. Typically, they receive little if any teacher education or professional development in literacy or strategy instruction. Naturally, they are reluctant to provide instruction in areas outside their expertise. Remediating students' reading, writing, and strategic deficiencies also takes time away from teaching students to think like scientists, historians, mathematicians, and other types of scholars. When a class period lasts 40 minutes, content area teachers logically prioritize teaching content over skills and strategies.

The kind of e.i. that could be provided in the content areas does not necessarily require an extensive amount of specialized training or instructional time. Pressley (2000), for example, identified and recommended a set of relatively manageable and straightforward strategies for helping students comprehend all sorts of texts. These are similar to the before–during–after reading strategies discussed in Chapter 8. They include prereading activities (e.g., preteaching unfamiliar vocabulary found in the text, making predictions, and pointing out salient text features), during-reading strategies (e.g., visualizing and stopping to check a dictionary or encyclopedia), and after-reading activities (e.g., summarizing and restating the text's main points, identifying confusing points, and verifying predictions). In short, content area teachers can provide explicit strategy instruction when students are having trouble making sense of particular reading materials, completing writing tasks, or performing well on tests and quizzes.

Conclusions

Improving the learning experiences of diverse learners requires the integration of a range of teaching strategies. Although what is viewed as effective instruction for inclusive classrooms continues to be refined, this book presents an e.i. framework that holds promise for increasing the academic performance of many students across grade levels and content areas. Explicit instruction often constitutes teaching "against the grain" of current educational thinking. However, e.i. should be used appropriately and strategically to help all students realize the standards and goals set by modern curricula and pedagogy: learning that occurs in a community of active learners who are increasingly strategic, self-regulated, and self-directed.

As teachers become more comfortable with the e.i. framework, they can expect to feel more capable of meeting the needs of all students in their classrooms and be more successful in doing so. As a result, students will be more motivated and successful learners. The strategies presented in this book may seem simple in theory; however, they are not necessarily easy to implement. It is critical that teachers working with this diverse population of students collaborate and share ideas. Only through such a process can teachers hope to improve instruction and promote student achievement in an inclusive environment.

REFERENCES

Adams, M. J. (1990). Phonics and beginning reading instruction. Champaign, IL: University of Illinois Press.

Adams, M. J. (1998). Beginning to read. Cambridge, MA: MIT Press.

Alverman, D. E. (1981). The compensatory effect of graphic organizers on descriptive text. Journal of Educational Research, 75, 44–48.

Anderson, R. C., Hiebert, E. H., Scott, J. A., & Wilkinson, A. G. (1985). Becoming a nation of readers: The report of the commission on reading. Washington, DC: National Institute of Education.

Anderson, J. R., Corbett, A. T., Koedinger, K. R., & Pelletier, R. (1995). Cognitive tutors: Lessons learned. Journal of the Learning Sciences, 4, 167–207.

Anderson, J. R., Reder, L. M., & Simon, H. A. (1996). Situated learning and education. Educational Researcher, 25(4), 5–11.

Anderson, L. M., Evertson, C. M., & Brophy, J. E. (1979). En experimental study of effective teaching in first grade reading groups. Elementary School Journal, 79, 193–223.

Anderson, R. J., Spiro, R. C., & Montague, W. E. (Eds.). (1984). Schooling and the acquisition of knowledge. Hillsdale, NJ: Lawrence Erlbaum Associates.

Ausubel, D. P. (1960). The use of advance organizers in the learning and retention of meaningful verbal material. Journal of Educational Psychology, 51, 267–272.

Ausubel, D. P., Novak, J. D., & Hanesian, J. (1978). Educational psychology: A cognitive view. New York: Holt, Rinehart and Winston.

Bauman, J. (1984). The effectiveness of a direct instruction paradigm for teaching main idea comprehension. Reading Research Quarterly, 20, 93–115.

Becker, W. C., Engleman, S., Carnine, D., & Rhine, R. (1981). The Direct Instruction model. In R. Rhine (Ed.), Making schools more effective: New directions from Follow Through (pp. 95–154). New York: Academic Press.

Biemiller, A. (2001). Teaching vocabulary: Early, direct, and sequential. American Educator, 25, 24–28, 47.

Bentley, J. L., & Conley, M. W. (1992). Making connections between substance abuse and literacy difficulties. Journal of Reading, 35, 386–389.

Berninger, V., Vaughan, K., Abbott, R., Brooks, A., Begay, K., Curin, G., et al. (2000). Language-based spelling instruction: Teaching children to make multiple connections between spoken and written words. Learning Disability Quarterly, 23, 117–135.

Bettencourt, E., Gillett, M., Gall, M., & Hull, R. (1983). Effects of teacher enthusiasm training on student on-task behavior and achievement. American Educational Research Journal, 20, 435–450.

Billingsley, B. S., & Wildman, T. M. (1984). Question generation and reading comprehension. Learning Disability Research, 4, 36–44.

Bond, G. R., & Dykstra, R. (1997). The cooperative research program in first-grade reading instruction. Reprinted in Reading Research Quarterly, 32, 348–427.

Bowers, P. G. (1993). Text reading and rereading: Predictors of fluency beyond word recognition. Journal of Reading behavior, 25, 133–153.

Brigham, F. J., Scruggs, T. E., & Mastropieri, M. A. (1992). Teacher enthusiasm in learning disabilities classrooms: Effects on learning and behavior. Learning Disabilities Research and Practice, 7, 68–73.

Brophy, J. (1983). Conceptualizing student motivation. Educational Psychologist, 18, 200–215.

Brophy, J., & Good, T. L. (1986). Teacher behavior and student achievement. In M. C. Wittrock (Ed.), Handbook of research on teaching (3rd ed., pp. 328–375). New York: Macmillan.

Brown, A. (1994). The advancement of learning. Educational Researcher, 28(8), 4–12.

Bruner, J. S. (1961). The art of discovery. Harvard Educational Review, 31, 21–32.

Carnine, D., Silbert, J., & Kameenui, E. (1997). Direct instruction reading (3rd ed.). Upper Saddle River, NJ: Prentice Hall.

Carr, J. F., & Harris, D. E. (2001). Succeeding with standards: Linking, curriculum, assessment, and action planning. Alexandria, VA: Association for Supervision and Curriculum Development.

Catts, H. W., Gillispie, M., Leonard, L. B., Kail, R. V., & Miller, C. A. (2002). The role of speed of processing, rapid naming, and phonological awareness in reading achievement. Journal of Learning Disabilities, 35, 510–525.

Chall, J. (1967). Learning to read: The great debate. New York: McGraw-Hill.

Chall, J. (1996). Stages of reading development. New York: McGraw-Hill.

Christensen, F. (1963). A generative rhetoric of the sentence. In The sentence and the paragraph. Urbana, IL: National Council of Teachers of English.

Christensen, F. (1965). A generative rhetoric of the paragraph. College Composition and Communication, 16, 144–156.

Cook, L. K., & Mayer, R. E. (1983). Reading strategies training for meaningful learning from prose. In M. Pressley & J. Levin (Eds.), Cognitive strategy research: Educational applications (pp. 448–456). New York: Springer-Verlag.

Cunningham, A. E. (1990). Explicit versus implicit instruction in phonemic awareness. Journal of Experimental Child Psychology, 50, 429–444.

Cunningham, P. M. (1995). Phonics they use: Words for reading and writing (2nd ed.). New York: Harper Collins.

Cunningham, P. M., Hall, D. P., & Sigmon, C. M. (2000). The teacher's guide to the four blocks: A multimethod, multilevel framework for grades 1–3. Greensboro, NC: Carson Dellosa Publishing Company.

Davidson, M., & Jenkins, J. R. (1994). Effects of phonemic processes on word reading and spelling. Journal of Educational Research, 148–157.

DeCecco, J. P. (1968). The psychology of learning and instruction: educational psychology. Upper Saddle River, NJ: Prentice Hall.

Deno, S. L. (1987). Curriculum-based measurement. Teaching Exceptional Children, 20, 41.

Deshler, D., Ellis, E. S., & Lenz, B. K. (1996). Teaching adolescents with learning disabilities: Strategies and methods. Baltimore: Brookes.

Deshler, D. D., & Schumaker, J. B. (1988). An instructional model for teaching students how to learn. In J. L. Graden, J. E. Zins, & M. J. Curtis (Eds.), Alternative educational delivery systems: Enhancing instructional options for all students (pp. 391–411). Washington, DC: National Association of School Psychologists.

Duffy, G. G., Roehler, L. R., Sivan, E., Rackliffe, G., Book, C., Meloth, M., et al. (1988). Effects of explaining the mental processing associated with using reading strategies on the awareness and achievement of low-group third grade readers. Reading Research Quarterly, 22, 347–368.

Edformation, Inc. (2006). Assessment and improvement monitoring systems (AIMSweb). Eden Prairie, MN: Author.

Ellis, E. S. (1989). A metacognitive intervention for increasing class participation. Learning Disabilities Focus, 5, 36–36.

Ellis, E. S. (1993). Integrative strategy instruction: A potential model for teaching content area subjects to adolescents with learning disabilities. Journal of Learning Disabilities, 26, 358–383.

Engelmann, S. (1980). Toward the design of faultless instruction: The theoretical basis of concept analysis. Educational Technology, 20, 28–36.

Engelmann, S., & Bruner, E. (1998). Reading mastery I. Chicago: Science Research Associates.

Engelmann, S., & Carnine, D. (1982). Theory of instruction: Principles and applications. New York: Irvington.

Englert, C. S., & Raphael, T. E. (1989). Developing successful writers through cognitive strategy instruction. In J. Brophy (Ed.), Advances in research on teaching (Vol. 1, pp. 105–151). Newark, NJ: JAI Press.

Espin, C. A., Busch, T. W., Shin, J., & Kruschwitz, R. (2001). Curriculum-based measurement in the content areas: Validity of vocabulary matching as an indicator of performance in social studies. Learning Disabilities Research and Practice, 16, 142–151.

Espin, C. A., & Foegen, A. (1996). Validity of general outcome measures for predicting secondary students' performance on content-area tasks. Exceptional Children, 62, 497–514.

Evans, M. A., & Carr, T. H. (1985). Cognitive abilities, conditions of learning, and the early development of reading skill. Reading Research Quarterly, 20, 327–350.

Fabre, T. (1984). The application of direct instruction in special education: An annotated bibliography. Unpublished manuscript.

Felton, R. H., & Pepper, P. P. (1995). Early identification and intervention of phonological deficits in kindergarten and early elementary children at-risk for reading disability. School Psychology Review, 24, 405–414.

Fisher, J., & Berliner, D. (1985). Perspectives on instructional time. New York: Longman.

Fisher, C., Berliner, D., Filby, N., Marliave, R., Cahen, L., & Dishaw, M. (1980). Teaching behaviors, academic learning time, and student achievement: An overview. In C. Denham & A. Lieberman (Eds.), Time to learn (pp. 7–32). Washington, DC: National Institute of Education.

Foegen, A. (2000). Technical adequacy of general outcome measures for middle school mathematics. Diagnostique, 25, 175–203.

Foegen, A., & Deno, S. L. (2001). Identifying growth indicators for low-achieving students in middle school mathematics. Journal of Special Education, 35, 4–16.

Foorman, B. R., Francis, D. J., Fletcher, J. M., Schatschneider, C., & Mehta, P. (1998). The role of instruction in learning to read: Preventing reading failure in at-risk children. Journal of Educational Psychology, 90, 37–55.

Foorman, B. R., & Torgesen, J. (2001). Critical elements of classroom and small-group instruction promote reading success in all children. Learning Disabilities Research and Practice, 16, 203–212.

Francis, D. J., et al. (1996). Developmental lag versus deficit models of reading disability: A longitudinal, individual growth curves analysis. Journal of Educational Psychology, 88, 3–17.

Fuchs, L. S., & Fuchs, D. (1998). Treatment validity: A unifying concept for reconceptualizing the identification of learning disabilities. Learning Disabilities Research and Practice, 13, 204–219.

Fuchs, L. S., & Fuchs, D. (2001). Using assessment data to account for and promote strong outcomes for students with disabilities. In D. Hallahan & B. Keough (Eds.), Research and global perspectives in learning disabilities: Essays in honor of William Cruickshank (pp. 93–110). Mahwah, NJ: Lawrence Erlbaum Associates.

Fuchs, D., Mathes, P. G., & Fuchs, L. S. (1995). Peabody peer assisted learning strategies (PALS): Reading methods. Nashville, TN: Peabody College, Vanderbilt University.

Gage, N. L., & Berliner, D. (1988). Educational psychology. Boston: Houghton Mifflin.

Gage, N. L., & Needels, M. C. (1989). Process-product research on teaching: A review of criticisms. Elementary School Journal, 89, 253–300.

Gagne, R., & Briggs, L. (1979). Principles of instructional design (2nd ed). New York: Holt, Rinehard, & Winston.

Gagne, R. M., Briggs, L. J., & Wager, W. W. (1992). The principles of instructional design. Fort Worth, TX: Harcourt Brace Jovanovich College Publishers.

Gagne, R. M., & Medsker, K. L. (1996). The conditions of learning: Training applications. Fort Worth, TX: Harcourt Brace College Publishers.

Gansle, K. A., Noell, G. H., VanDerHeyden, A. M., Naquin, G. M., & Slider, N. J. (2002). Moving beyond total words written: The reliability, criterion validity, and time cost of alternative measures for curriculum based measurement in writing. School Psychology Review, 31, 477–497.

Gardner, R., Heward, W. L., & Grossi, T. A. (1994). Effects of response cards on student participation and academic achievement: A systematic replication with inner-city students during whole-class science instruction. Journal of Applied Behavioral Analysis, 27, 63–71.

Gersten, R. (1985). Direct Instruction with special education students: A review of evaluation research. Journal of Special Education, 19, 41–58.

Gersten, R., Carnine, D. W., & Williams, P. B. (1982). Measuring implementation of a structured educational model in an urban school district: An observational approach. Educational Evaluation and Policy Analysis, 4, 67–79.

Good, T. L., & Brophy, J. E. (2007). Looking in classrooms (10th ed). Boston: Allyn & Bacon.

Good, R. H., & Kaminski, R. A. (2003). Dynamic indicators of basic early literacy skills (DIBELS). Eugene: University of Oregon Center on Teaching and Learning.

Good, T. L., & Grouws, D. A. (1977). Teaching effects: A process-product study in a fourth grade mathematics classroom. Journal of Teacher Education, 28(3), 49–54.

Good, T. L., & Grouws, D. A. (1979). The Missouri Mathematics Effectiveness Project: An experimental study in fourth grade classrooms. Journal of Educational Psychology, 71, 355–372.

Goodman, K. S. (2005). What's whole in whole language. Muskegon, MI: RDR Books.

Graham, S. (1999). Handwriting and spelling instruction for students with learning disabilities: A review. Learning Disability Quarterly, 22, 78–98.

Graham, S. (2006). Strategy instruction and the teaching of writing: A meta-analysis. In C. A. MacArthur, S. Graham, & J. Fitzgerald (Eds.), Handbook of writing research (pp. 187–207). New York: Guilford.

Graham, S., Berninger, V., Abbott, R., Abbott, S., & Whitaker, D. (1997). Role of mechanics in composing of elementary school students: A new methodological approach. Journal of Educational Psychology, 89, 170–182.

Graham, S., & Harris, K. (2005). Writing better: Effective strategies for teaching students with learning difficulties. Baltimore: Brookes.

Graham, S., Harris, K., & MacArthur, C. (2006). Explicitly teaching struggling writers: Strategies for mastering the writing process. Intervention in School and Clinic, 41, 290–294.

Haynes, T., & Jennings, C. (in press). Listening and speaking: Essential ingredients for struggling writers.

Heward, W. L. (1994). Three "low tech" strategies for increasing the frequency of student response during group instruction. In R. Gardner III, D. M.

Sainato, J. O. Cooper, T. E. Heron, W. L. Heward, J. Eshleman, et al. (Eds.), Behavior analysis in education: Focus on measurably superior instruction (pp. 283–320). Pacific Grove, CA: Brooks/Cole.

Honig, B. (1995). How should we teach our children to read? Minutes of the Superintendent's Reading Task Force, May 19, 1995.

Honig, B. (1996). Teaching our children to read. Thousand Oaks, CA: Sage Publications.

Hunter, M. (1982). Mastery teaching. El Segundo, CA: TIP Publications.

Hunter, M. (1994). Enhancing teaching. New York: Macmillan.

Karp, K. S., & Voltz, D. L. (2000). Weaving mathematical instructional strategies into inclusive settings. Intervention in School and Clinic, 35, 206–215.

King, A. (1990). Improving lecture comprehension: Effects of a metacognitive strategy. Applied Cognitive Psychology, 4, 1–16.

Lapp, D., & Flood, J. (1998). Where's the phonics? Making the case (again) for integrated code instruction (point-counterpoint). The Reading Teacher, 50, 96–98.

Lenchner, O., Gerber, M., & Routh, D. (1990). Phonological awareness tasks as predictors of decoding ability: Beyond segmentation. Journal of Learning Disabilities, 23, 240–247.

Lyon, G. R. (1999). The NICHD research program in reading development, reading disorders and reading instruction: A summary of research findings. New York: National Center for Learning Disabilities.

Marzano, R. J., & Pickering, D. J. (2005). Building academic vocabulary. Alexandria, VA: Association for Supervision and Curriculum Development.

Mastropieri, M. A., & Scruggs, T. E. (1997). Promoting inclusion in secondary classrooms. Learning Disability Quarterly, 24, 265–284.

Mastropieri, M. A., & Scruggs, T. E. (2000). The inclusive classrooms: Strategies for effective instruction. Upper Saddle River, NJ: Prentice Hall.

Mayer, R. E. (1979). Can advance organizers influence meaningful learning? Review of Educational Research, 49, 371–383.

Meichenbaum, D., & Beimiller, A. (1998). Nurturing independent learners: Helping students take charge of their own learning. Boston: Brookline.

Mercer, C. D., Jordan, L., & Miller, S. P. (1996). Constructivistic math instruction for diverse learners. Learning Disabilities Research and Practice, 11, 147–156.

Mercer, C. D., Lane, H., Jordan, L., Allsopp, D. H., & Eisele, M. R. (1996). Empowering teachers and students with instructional choices in inclusive settings. Remedial and Special Education, 17, 226–236.

Meyer, M. S., & Felton, R. H. (1999). Repeated reading to enhance fluency: Old approaches and new directions. Annals of Dyslexia, 49, 283–306.

Miller, C. D., & Mercer, A. R. (1997). Educational aspects of mathematics disabilities. Journal of Learning Disabilities, 30, 47–56.

Moats, L. (1995). The missing foundation in teacher preparation. American Educator, 19(9), 43–51.

Moats, L. (1999). Teaching reading is rocket science: What expert teachers of reading should know and be able to do. Washington, DC: American Federation of Teachers.

Montague, M. (1997). Cognitive strategy instruction in mathematics for students with learning disabilities. Journal of Learning Disabilities, 30(2), 164–177.

Montague M. (1998). Math instruction in diverse classrooms. In K. R. Harris, S. Graham, & D. Deshler (Eds.), Teaching every child every day: Learning in diverse schools and classrooms. Cambridge, MA: Brookline Books.

Nagy, W. E., & Herman, P. A. (1987). Breadth and depth of vocabulary knowledge: Implications for acquisition and instruction. In M. McKeown & M. Curtis (Eds.), The nature of vocabulary acquisition (pp. 19–35). Hillsdale, NJ: Erlbaum Associates.

National Assessment of Educational Progress. (2007). U.S. Department of Education, Institute of Education Sciences. Retrieved January 21, 2008, from http://nationsreportcard.gov/reading_2007/r0012.asp

National Institute of Child Health and Human Development. (2000). Report of the National Reading Panel: Teaching children to read: An evidence-based assessment. Washington, D.C.

No Child Left Behind. (2002). Retrieved September 27, 2004, from http://ww.ed.gov/policy/elsec/leg/esea02.html

Papert, S. (1980). Mindstorms: Children, computers, and powerful ideas. New York: Basic Books.

Perie, M., Grigg, W., & Donahue, P. (2005). The nation's report card: Reading 2005 (NCES 2006–451). Washington, DC: U.S. Department of Education.

Pinnell, G. S., Lyons, C. A., DeFord, D. E., Bryk, A. S., & Seltzer, M. (1994). Comparing instructional models for the literacy education of high-risk first graders. Reading Research Quarterly, 29, 8–39.

Pintrich, P. R., & DeGroot, E. V. (1990). Motivational and self-regulated learning components of classroom academic performance. Journal of Educational Psychology, 82, 32–40.

Popham, W. J. (2001). The truth about testing: An educator's call to action. Alexandria, VA: Association for Supervision and Curriculum Development.

Pressley, M. (1998). Reading instruction that works: The case for balanced instruction. New York: Guilford.

Pressley, M. (2000). What should comprehension instruction be the instruction of? In M. Kamil et al. (Eds.), Handbook of reading research (Vol. 3, pp. 545–562). Mahwah, NJ: Lawrence Erlbaum Associates.

Pressley, M., & McCormick, C. (1995). Cognition, teaching, and assessment. New York: Harper Collins.

Pressley, M., Burkell, L., Cariglia-Bull, T., Lysynchuk, L., McGoldrick, J. A., Schneider, B., et al. (1995). Cognitive strategy instruction (2nd ed.). Cambridge, MA: Brookline.

Pressley, M., Forrest-Pressley, D., Elliott-Faust, D. L., & Miller, G. E. (1985). Children's use of cognitive strategies, how to teach strategies, and what to do if they can't be taught. In M. Pressley & C. J. Brainerd (Eds.), Cognitive learning and memory in children (pp. 1–47). New York: Springer-Verlag.

Pressley, M., Mohan, L., Fingeret, L., Reffitt, K., & Bogaert, L. R. (2007). Writing instruction in engaging and effective elementary settings. In C. MacArthur, S. Graham, & J. Fitzgerald (Eds.), Best practices in writing instruction: Solving problems in the teaching of literacy (pp. 13–27). New York: Guilford.

Raphael, T. E. (1986). Teaching question-answer relationships. The Reading Teacher, 39, 516–520.

Readence, J. E., Bean, T. W., & Baldwin, R. S. (2004). Content area literacy: An integrated approach. Dubuque, IA: Kendall/Hunt.

Reutzel, D. R., & Hollingsworth, P. M. (1988). Whole language and the practitioner. Academic Therapy, 23, 405–416.

Richardson, V. (1996). The role of attitudes and beliefs in learning to teach. In J. Sikula (Ed.), Handbook of research on teacher education (2nd ed., pp. 102–119). New York: Macmillan.

Rosenshine, B. (1983) . Teaching functions in instructional programs. Elementary School Journal, 83, 335–351.

Rosenshine, B. (1995). Advances in research on instruction. Journal of Educational Research, 88, 262–268.

Rosenshine, B. (1997). Advances in research on instruction. In E. J. Lloyd, E. J. Kameanui, & D. Chard (Eds.), Issues in educating students with disabilities (pp. 197–221). Mahwah, NJ: Lawrence Erlbaum Associates.

Rosenshine, B., Meister, C., & Chapman, S. (1996). Teaching students to generate questions: A review of the intervention studies. Review of Educational Research, 66, 181–221.

Rosenshine, B., & Stevens, R. (1984). Research on teaching reading. In P. D. Pearson (Ed.), Handbook of research on reading (pp. 745–799). New York: Longman.

Royer, J. M., & Sinatra, G. M. (1994). A cognitive theoretical approach to reading diagnostics. Educational Psychology Review, 6, 81–114.

Saddler, B. (2005). Sentence combining: A sentence-level writing intervention. The Reading Teacher, 58, 468–471.

Saddler, B., & Graham, S. (2005). The effects of peer-assisted sentence combining instruction on the writing performance of more and less skilled young writers. Educational Psychology, 97, 43–54.

Samuels, S. J. (1981). Characteristics of exemplary reading programs. In J. Guthrie (Ed.), Comprehension and teaching: Research reviews (pp. 255–273). New York: Holt, Rinehart, & Winston.

Scardamalia, M., & Bereiter, C. (1985). Fostering the development of self-regulation in students' knowledge processing. In S. F. Chipman, J. W. Segal, & R. Glaser (Eds.), Thinking and learning skills: Research and open questions (pp. 563–578). Hillsdale, NJ: Lawrence Erlbaum Associates.

Schumaker, J. B., & Deshler, D. D. (1992). Validation of learning strategy interventions for students with LD: Results of programmatic research effort. In Y. L. Wong (Ed.), Contemporary intervention research in learning disabilities: An international perspective. New York: Springer-Verlag.

Schunk, D. H. (2003). Self-efficacy for reading and writing: Influence of modeling, goal-setting, and self-evaluation. Reading and Writing Quarterly, 19, 159–172.

Shankweiler, D., Lundquist, E., Katz, L., & Steubing, J. M. (1999). Comprehension and decoding: Patterns of association in children with reading difficulties. Scientific Studies of Reading, 3, 95–112.

Shaywitz, S. E., Escobar, M. D., Shaywitz, B. A., Fletcher, J. M., & Makuch, R. (1992). Distribution and temporal stability of dyslexia in an epidemiological sample of 414 children followed longitudinally. New England Journal of Medicine, 326, 145–150.

Silbert, J., Stein, M., & Carnine, D. (1997). Designing effective mathematics instruction: A direct instruction approach (3rd ed.). Upper Saddle River, NJ: Prentice Hall.

Singer, H., & Donlan, D. (1982). Active comprehension: Problem-solving schema with question generation of complex short stories. Reading Research Quarterly, 17, 166–186.

Skinner, B. (1968). The technology of teaching. New York: Appleton-Crofts.

Skinner, E. A., & Belmont, M. J. (1993). Motivation in the classroom: Reciprocal effects of teacher behavior and student engagement across the school year. Journal of Educational Psychology, 85, 571–581.

Slavin, R. E. (2000). Educational psychology: Theory and practice (6th ed.). Upper Saddle River, NJ: Prentice Hall.

Smith, L. R. (1985). Teacher clarifying behaviors: Effects of student achievement and perceptions. Journal of Experimental Education, 53, 162–169.

Smith, L. R., & Land, M. L. (1981). Low-inference verbal behaviors related to teacher clarity. Journal of Classroom Interaction, 17, 37–42.

Snow, C. (2002). Reading for understanding: Toward an R&D program in reading comprehension. Santa Monica, CA: RAND.

Speece, D. L., & Case, L. (2001). Classification in context: An alternative to identifying early reading disability. Journal of Educational Psychology, 93, 735–749.

Stahl, S. A., & Miller, P. D. (1989). Whole language and language experience approaches for beginning reading: A quantitative research synthesis. Review of Educational Research, 59(1), 87–116.

Stahl, S. A., & Shiel, T. G. (1992). Teaching meaning vocabulary: Productive approaches for poor readers. Reading and Writing Quarterly, 8, 223–241.

Stanovich, K. E. (1980). Toward an interactive-compensatory model of individual differences in the development of reading fluency. Reading Research Quarterly, 13, 32–71.

Stanovich, K. E., & West, R. F. (1989). Exposure to print and orthographic processing. Reading Research Quarterly, 24, 402–433.

Stebbins, L. B., St. Pierre, R. G., Proper, E. C., Anderson, R. B., & Cerva, T. R. (1977). Education as experimentation: A planned variation model. Cambridge, MA: Abt Associates.

Steffe, L., & Gale, J. (Eds.). (1995). Constructivism in education. Hillsdale, NJ: Lawrence Erlbaum Associates.

Strickland, D. (1998). Teaching phonics today: A primer for educators. Newark, DE: International Reading Association.

Sulzby, E. (1985). Children's reading of favorite storybooks: A developmental study. Reading Research Quarterly, 20, 458–481.

Swanson, H. L. (1999). Reading research for students with LD: A meta-analysis of intervention outcomes. Journal of Learning Disabilities, 32, 504–532.

Swanson, H. L. (2001). Searching for the best model for instructing students with learning disabilities. Focus on Exceptional Children, 34, 1–15.

Tarver, S. G. (1992). Direct instruction. In W. Stainback & S. Stainback (Eds.), Controversial issues confronting special education: Divergent perspectives (2nd ed., pp. 143–165). Boston: Allyn & Bacon.

Tomlinson, C. A. (2004). The differentiated classroom: Responding to the needs of all learners. Upper Saddle River, NJ: Prentice Hall.

Torgesen, J. K. (1985). Memory processes in reading disabled children. Journal of Learning Disabilities, 18, 350–357.

Traub, J. (1999). Better by design? A consumer's guide to school reform. The Thomas B. Fordham Foundation. Available: http://www.edexcellence.net/library/bbd/better_by_design.html

U.S. Department of Education. (2002). Twenty-fourth annual report to Congress on implementation of the Individuals with Disabilities Education Act. Washington, DC: Author.

Vaughn, S. (2003). Response to instruction as a means of identifying students with reading/learning disabilities. Exceptional Children, 69, 391–409.

Vellutino, F., Scanlon, D., Sipay, E., Small, S., Pratty, A., Chen, R., et al. (1996). Cognitive profiles of difficult-to-remediate and readily remediated poor readers: Early intervention as a vehicle for distinguishing between cognitive and experiential deficits as basic causes of specific reading disability. Journal of Educational Psychology, 88, 601–638.

Viorst, J. (1987). Alexander, who used to be rich last Sunday. New York: Aladdin.

Wade, S., & Moje, E. (2000). The role of text in classroom learning. In M. Kamil et al. (Eds.), Handbook of reading research (Vol. 3, pp. 609–628). Mahwah, NJ: Lawrence Erlbaum Associates.

Wagner, R., & Torgesen, J. K. (1987). The nature of phonological processing and its causal role in the acquisition of reading skills. Psychological Bulletin, 101, 192–212.

Wagner, R., Torgesen, J. K., Laughon, P., Simmons, K., & Rashotte, C. A. (1993). Development of young readers phonological processing abilities. Journal of Educational Psychology, 85, 83–103.

Weaver, C. (1998). Toward a balanced approach to reading in reconsidering a balanced approach to reading. Urbana, IL: National Council of Teachers of English.

Weinert, F. E., & Helmke, A. (1995). Interclassroom differences in instructional quality and interindividual differences in cognitive development. Educational Psychologist, 30, 15–20.

Weinstein, C. E., & Underwood, V. L. (1985). Learning strategies: The how of learning. In J. Segal, S. Chipman, & R. Glaser (Eds.), Thinking and learning skills (pp. 241–258). Hillsdale, NJ: Lawrence Erlbaum Associates.

Wiggins, G. P. (1993). Assessing student performance: Exploring the purpose and limits of testing. San Francisco: Jossey-Bass.

Winters, C. A. (1997). Learning disabilities, crime, delinquency, and special education placement. Adolescence, 32, 451–462.

Wittrock, M. C. (1978). Education and the cognitive processes of the brain. In J. S. Chall & A. F. Mirsky (Eds.), Education and the brain (pp. 61–102). Seventy-seventh yearbook of the National Society for the Study of Education (Part II). Chicago: University of Chicago Press.

Woodward, J., & Baxter, J. (1997). The effects of an innovative approach to mathematics on academically low achieving students in mainstreamed settings. Exceptional Children, 63, 373–388.

Wolf, M., & Katzir-Cohen, T. (2001). Reading fluency and its intervention. Scientific Studies of Reading, 5, 211–238.

Wong, B. Y. L. (1986). Metacognition and special education: A review of a view. Journal of Special Education, 20, 9–29.

Wong, B. Y. L. (1996). The ABC's of learning disabilities. San Diego, CA: Academic Press.

APPENDIX A
Explicit Instruction Lesson Plan Format

Date: **Subject:**   **Grade:**
Lesson topic: **Class/group size:**
Learning objective (performance, conditions, criterion):

State curriculum standards:

I. Core and Supplemental Materials

I need: Students need:

II. Context for Learning

    a. Organization of students (e.g., small groups, large group, etc.)
    b. Prelesson assessment date: On what prelesson assessment data is this lesson based?

Prelesson assessment data:
Individualized education plan (IEP) link (If the student has an IEP, how does this lesson link to IEP goals/objectives?):

III. Preinstructional Set

    a. Gain students' attention
    b. Inform students of learning objective(s):
    c. Use informed instruction: This is important to know because . . .

IV. Prepare Students for Instructional Content

(PLAN 1)

    a. Review of prerequisite skills (if applicable):
    b. Activate prior knowledge (if applicable):
    c. Preteach key vocabulary (if applicable):

V. Instruction

    a. Cognitive modeling
    b. Guided practice
    c. Check student understanding
    d. Independent practice

How will you address it if reteaching is necessary for some students?

VI. Assessment

How will you know whether students have met your learning objective?

* Assessment activities must be concrete and tangible.

VII. Closure

Active review:
Organize/transition (e.g., Students put their work in their language arts folder and return it to the bin. Transition to next lesson/activity).

Homework or follow-up:

VIII. Notes for Modifications/Accommodations and Paraprofessional Support

During explicit instruction (e.g., visuals, procedural prompts, peer-assisted learning strategies, technology, etc.):

Paraprofessional support:

Additional individual student needs:

APPENDIX B
Weekly Block Plans for Explicit Instruction

Reading	Language Arts	Math
CCCS: Demonstrate comprehension 3.2-8 Obj: SWBAT read and understand the story "Crazy Critters." Pro: Each student will be assigned a part in the script. Students will read story with emotions. Class will discuss. Ma: Story Ev: Class participation	CCCS: Concise organized speech 3.2 Obj: SWBAT review nouns and begin lesson on common and proper nouns. Pro: Class will review nouns orally. Students will copy definition of common and proper nouns. Class will complete text pages 108 to 109. Ma: Board, textbook, notebook Ev: Class participation, written work	CCCS: Solve problems for everyday experiences 4.1-11 Obj: SWBAT use greater-than and less-than symbols correctly. Pro: Teacher will review comparing numbers. Students will be able to complete teacher-made worksheet and correct with class. Ma: Teacher-made worksheet Ev: Class participation, worksheet
Obj: SWBAT read and understand the story "The Girl Fish." Pro: Each student will be assigned a part in the script. Students will read story with emotions. Class will discuss. Ma: Story Ev: Class participation	Obj: SWBAT understand common and proper nouns. Pro: Teacher will review definitions. Class will complete text pages 186 to 187 and correct together in class. Ma: Board, textbook Ev: Completed class work	Obj: SWBAT use greater-than and less-than symbols correctly. Pro: Teacher will have students come to board and complete given problems. Students will complete simple addition problems and then use symbols to compare answers. Ma: Board, worksheet Ev: Completed worksheet
Obj: SWBAT read and understand the story "Coughy," the dwarf Snow White never told you about." Pro: Each student will be assigned a part in the script. Students will read story with emotions. Class will discuss. Ma: Story Ev: Class participation	Obj: SWBAT identify common and proper nouns. Pro: Teacher will review. Students will work in pairs to complete workbook pages 22 to 23. Class will correct together. Ma: Workbook Ev: Completed classwork	Obj: SWBAT use greater-than and less-than symbols correctly. Pro: Teacher will review using the board. Students will complete worksheet. Ma: Board, worksheet Ev: Completed classwork

(continued)

Reading	Language Arts	Math
Obj: SWBAT read and understand the story "Three Billy Goats Gruff." Pro: Each student will be assigned a part in the script. Students will read story with emotions. Class will discuss. Ma: Story Ev: TO through class participation	Obj: SWBAT identify proper nouns. Pro: Teacher will review and compare common and proper nouns. Students will complete workbook pages 24 to 25. Ma: Workbook Ev; Completed classwork	Obj: SWBAT use greater-than and less-than symbols correctly. Pro: Students will use greater-than and less-than symbols to compare numbers in the ten thousands. Ma: Worksheet, board Ev: Completed worksheet

Note: Obj = learning objective; Pro = procedure; Ma = materials; Ev = evaluation.

APPENDIX C
Explicit Instruction Checklist

OBJECTIVES

_____ The learning objective includes a performance, conditions, and criterion.

_____ The learning goals lend themselves to explicit instruction (e.g., basic or component skill and well-defined content that all students must master).

_____ The objective(s) effectively match:

_____ student objectives _____ guided practice _____ assessment
_____ instruction _____ independent practice

PREINSTRUCTIONAL SET

_____ Effective attention-gaining strategies are used.

_____ Objectives that students are told match the teacher's learning objectives.

_____ Objectives are phrased in terms of what students will be able to *do* when the lesson is complete.

_____ Appropriate lesson details are provided.

PREPARING STUDENTS FOR INSTRUCTIONAL CONTENT

_____ Students' prior knowledge is accessed/activated by means of a pencil-and-paper activity (list, questionnaire, K-W-L) or direct questioning activity that requires *active participation by all students.*

_____ Plans are included for responding to/connecting students' prior knowledge to the current objective and/or

_____ Plans are included for visual organization of prior knowledge (e.g., use of chart, web, overhead, or other visual).

_____ Plans include a specific strategy for brief practice/review relevant to the current objective, using a strategy that fosters *active participation by all students* (e.g., group problem solving, individual application, or working with peers).

INSTRUCTION

_____ Cognitive model is for *learning* rather than directions for an activity (e.g., a skill/strategy rather than a game).

_____ Modeling is explicit and broken down into appropriate steps (e.g., thinking before, during, and after).

_____ Teacher completely models the skill/strategy at least one time first, followed by teacher modeling with scaffolded student input.

_____ Students are given a useful mnemonic, strategy, or procedural prompt.

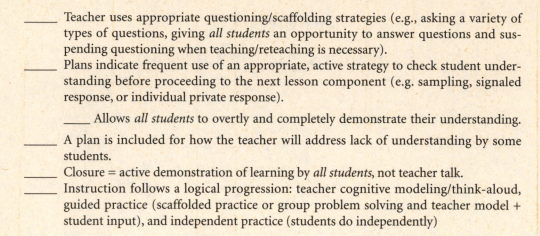

_____ Teacher uses appropriate questioning/scaffolding strategies (e.g., asking a variety of types of questions, giving *all students* an opportunity to answer questions and suspending questioning when teaching/reteaching is necessary).

_____ Plans indicate frequent use of an appropriate, active strategy to check student understanding before proceeding to the next lesson component (e.g. sampling, signaled response, or individual private response).

_____ Allows *all students* to overtly and completely demonstrate their understanding.

_____ A plan is included for how the teacher will address lack of understanding by some students.

_____ Closure = active demonstration of learning by *all students*, not teacher talk.

_____ Instruction follows a logical progression: teacher cognitive modeling/think-aloud, guided practice (scaffolded practice or group problem solving and teacher model + student input), and independent practice (students do independently)

INDEX

A

Acquisition, 19
  versus mastery problems, 19
Activate prior knowledge, 62–64
  nonexamples of, 64
  strategies for, 63–64
Active engagement, 38
Active participation, 37–42
  Strategies for, 41
Assessment
  Data, deriving meaning from, 21
  Large scale assessment, 20
  Classroom assessment, 22
  Curriculum based
    assessment, 21–23
  Role in e.i., 19–20
Attention, gaining students' 50–54
  difficulty gaining, 53
  nonexamples of, 52
  strategies for, 51

B

Basic skills, 15–16
  matching assessment to basic skills
    in reading, writing, and math, 16
Blending , 88
Block plans, 127–128

C

Classroom assessment, 22
Closure, 76–78
  examples of closure activities, 77
  lesson closure summary sheet, 78
Cloze notes, 114
Cognitive modeling, 69–73
  nonexamples of, 73
Composition, 104
Comprehension. See Reading
  comprehension
Comprehensive reading instruction,
  85–86
Consolidation, 17–18
Content areas, e.i. in, 112–113
Continuum, learning and teaching, 17
Corrective feedback, 45
Curriculum based assessment, 21–22

D

Direct Instruction (D.I.), 5
  versus d.i., 5–8
Direct instruction (d.i.), 6–8
  versus D.I., 5–8

E

Elaboration, 115
Examples, importance of, 71

Explicit instruction, 8–13
  as an alternative to d.i. or learner-
    centered approaches, 9
  checklist for, 129–130
  contradictions of, 7–8
  framework, 13
  in literacy, 83
  planning for, 25–28
  role of assessment in, 19–20
  what is e.i.?, 10
  when is e.i. appropriate?, 28

F

Four blocks, 85
Fluency, 95–96

G

Guided practice, 73–76
  aligning with learning
    objectives, 74
  application based, 76
  examples of activities for, 74
  nonexamples, 75
  skill-based, 76

H

Handwriting, 102
  skills and strategies for, 103
Homework, 114

I

Independent practice, 75–76
Informed instruction, 55–58
Isolated sound recognition, 90

L

Large-scale assessment, 20
Learning strategies, 112, 115
Lesson planning
  for e.i., 28
  sample lesson plan format,
    125–126
  sample lesson plan
    mathematics, 110
    phonics lesson, 94
    reading comprehension, 100
Letter-sound recognition, 91
Literacy, e.i. in, 83

M

Mastery, 19
  versus acquisition problems, 19
Mathematics, e.i. in, 107–112
  sample lesson plan for, 110–112
Mnemonic strategies, 104
Model—lead—test approach, 108
Modeling. See cognitive modeling.

Monitoring
  student progress, 20
  student understanding, 43–45

N

National Reading Panel, 86
Nonexamples, importance of, 71–72
Notetaking, 114

O

Onset and rime, 89
Objectives
  informing students of, 54–56
  performance terms for, 27
  student-oriented, 55–56
  versus activities, 26
  writing correctly worded, 25–28

P

Pacing, 33
Paragraph shrinking, 98
Personal organization skills, 113
Planning for e.i., 25–28
  block plans, 127–128
  checklist for, 129–130
  lesson plan format for e.i.,
    125–126
  writing objectives for, 25–26
Performance terms, 27
Phonemic awareness, 86–87
  blending, 88
  instructional considerations
    for, 87
  isolated sound recognition, 90
  letter-sound association, 91
  onset and rime, 89
  rhyme, 88
  segmentation, 88
  sound deletion, 90
Phonics, 87
  instructional model, 93
  research-based conclusions
    about, 91
  sample lesson plan for, 94
  scope and sequence, 92
Practice, 18; 73–76
Pre-instructional set, 49–50
  gain students' attention, 50–54
  inform students of the lesson
    objective, 54–56
  use informed instruction, 55–58
Preteach key vocabulary, 66–67
Procedural prompts, 42–43; 109

Q

Question-answer relationships
  (QAR), 96–97

R

Reading, importance of e.i. in, 83–86
Reading comprehension, 96–98
  instructional model, 97
  sample lesson plan for, 100
Reading strategies for e.i., 99
Response to intervention (RtI), 16
Review
  in mathematics, 108
  previously learned skills, 64–66
Rhyme, 88

S

Scaffolding, 18
Segmentation, 88
Self-management skills. *See* personal organization skills.

Sentence combining, 104
Sentence expansion, 104
Sound deletion, 90
Spelling, 103–104
Student engagement variables, 39
  active participation, 39–42
  monitoring understanding, 43–45
  procedural prompts, 42–43
Study skills, 113–115

T

Teacher presentation variables, 30–34
  clarity, 30–32
  enthusiasm, 33–34
  interaction frame for, 31
  rate of presentation, 32–33

U

Understanding, 44–45
  giving corrective feedback, 45
  nonexamples of strategies for checking understanding, 45
  strategies for checking, 44–45

V

Verbal explanations, 71–72
Vocabulary, 92–93
  preteaching, 66–67

W

Written expression, 98–99
  self-regulation and self-instructional strategies for, 105